Innocent Blood

Innocent Blood

Graham Jooste
and
Roger Webster

SPEARHEAD

Dedicated to Colleen and Margaret

Published by Spearhead
An imprint of New Africa Books (Pty) Ltd.
99 Garfield Road
Claremont 7700
South Africa

(021) 674 4136
info@newafricabooks.co.za

First edition, first impression 2002

ISBN: 0-86486-532-5

Translation by Roger Webster and Graham Jooste
Editing by Michael Collins
Proofreading by Sean Fraser
Layout and design by Peter Stuckey
Cover design by Odette Marais
Origination by House Of Colours
Printing and binding by ABC Press, Cape Town

Contents

Introduction   9

Section 1
Executions in the Cape Colony

1. **Two Bags of Unslaked Lime**   17
2. **Rebels or Ordinary Soldiers?**   20
3. **The Military Courts**   25
4. **Illegal Executions**   30
    Hendrik Jacobus van Heerden, Charel Gerhardus Johannes
    Nienaber, Jan Petrus Nienaber and Johannes (Jan) Andries
    Nieuwoudt
5. **Hanged in Public**   36
    Cornelius Johannes Claassen, Johannes Petrus Coetzee and
    Frederick Abram Marais
6. **Burgersdorp, That 'Rebel Nest'**   45
    Petrus Willem Klopper
7. **'In the Sand of Graaff-Reinet ...'**   50
    Petrus Jacobus Fourie, Jan van Rensburg and
    Lodewyk Francois Stephanus Pfeiffer
8. **The Sins of Two Lost Boys**   57
    Daniël F Olwagen and Ignatius W Nel
9. **A Turn for Colesberg**   62
    Hendrik Petrus van Vuuren, Frederick Toy (Toe) and
    Hendrik Johan Veenstra

10. **The Destruction of the Lötter Commando**   70
Commandant Johannes Cornelius Lötter,
Pieter Jacobus Wolfaardt, Commandant Dirk C Breed,
Field-Cornet Wilhelm Stephanus Kruger and
Lieutenant Jacobus Gustavus Schoeman

11. **Captured in Khaki**   88
Piet de Ruyt, Cornelius Vermaas, Henry Rittenberg,
Arie van Onselen and John (Jack) Alexander Baxter

12. **The Brood of Andrew Murray**   96
Field-Cornet Willie Hofmeyer Louw

13. **Active in Arms**   103
Pieter Willem van Heerden, Nicolaas Francois van Wijk,
Johannes Hermanus Roux and Jacobus Francois Geldenhuys

14. **Two Fighters and a Traitor**   115
Lieutenant Piet Bester, Francois Edward Davis and
Lieutenant Izak Bartholomeus Liebenberg

15. **Executions of Coloured People**   129

16. **Attack on the Border Scouts Near Kenhardt**   133
Abraham Christiaan Jooste and Hendrik Lourens Jacobs

17. **The Siege of Mafeking**   140
Field-Cornet Arnoldus Renike and Louis Brink

18. **The Windmill Gallows of Vryburg**   142
Johannes Gert Wolfaardt Jansen,
Nicolaas Claassen Rautenbach, Field-Cornet Hermanus (Manie)
Kuhn and Johannes (Jurie) Kuhn

19. **An Ordinary Soldier and No Rebel**   149
Commandant Gideon Jacobus Scheepers

20. **The Forgotten One**   165
Francois Engelbertus du Randt

Section 2
Executions in the Republics

1. **The Plot to Abduct Lord Roberts**   179
   Hans Cordua
2. **'The Sympathetic Hero and Martyr'**   182
   Cornelis Broeksma
3. **Murder Under the White Flag and After Surrender**   188
   Field-Cornet Salmon van As, Pieter (Piet) Schuil,
   Jan Abraham Basson, TC Lombard and PC Fourie
4. **Murder**   197
   Christiaan Lodewicus Pienaar, Jacobus Johannes de Jager,
   Commandant RD van Schalkwyk and Jan Lewis
5. **Captured in Khaki**   202
   SJ (Fransie) Kruger, I Koen, Straus (Struis), C Steyn
6. **Oath Violation and High Treason**   204
   PR Krause, NT Venter, David Garnus Wernick,
   Renier Christiaan Upton, Vermaak
7. **The Execution of a Deserter – A Love Story**   207
   Trooper George Frederick Shaw
8. **Executions Without Trial**   209
   Breaker Morant and the Bushveld Carbineers,
   Gerhard C Kooijker, JF Vercuul, FGJ Potgieter,
   JJ Geiser, PJ Geiser (age 11), JC Greeling, Van Heerden,
   Van Buuren, Visser, Van den Berg, Baauwkens,
   WD Vahrmeyer, CPJ Smit, Logenaar, GK Westerhof,
   B Wouters, JJ du Preez (age 16), Pauskie, Reverend
   Carl August David Heese, Jan Dirk Grobler (age 13),
   Daniel Grobler, R van Staden, C van Staden (age 17) and
   R van Staden Jnr (age 11)

Conclusion   217
The Hague Convention

Appendix A   220
Rebels: Military Blue Book

Appendix B   221
Military Court Records

Appendix C   228
Statistics of Trials and Executions

Appendix D   230
Sources

Appendix E   236
Select Bibliography

Introduction

My interest in the conflict between the Boers and the British no doubt originated because I am half Boer and half British. On my paternal side, the family suffered the pains of the concentration camps, death and banishment. My mother is a Lancastrian by birth and my wife, Colleen, is of Irish extraction. Our home language is English and I completed my formal education at the South African Nautical College *General Botha* in Gordons Bay, part of my youth spent at sea in the mercantile marine. For many years Colleen and I have visited battlefields, monuments and historical areas in search of the forgotten graves of both Boer and Brit. When I discovered that a distant relative, Abraham Jooste, had died before a firing squad in Kenhardt, my interest in these matters took a more definite course.

Research into the executions of the Cape rebels has taken me into the far corners of the former Cape Colony. Museums, gaols, cemeteries, farms and finally the National Archives in Cape Town helped inform my insatiable interest. These were the men who paid the ultimate price during the turmoil of the Boer commandos' excursions into the British-held Cape Colony.

During one of my visits to Aliwal North, I visited the Concentration Camp Memorial in search of the grave of Izak Liebenberg, and came across a person inspecting the inlaid tombstones methodically and carefully. To my amazement I discovered that he was searching for details of Liebenberg as well, but had been unsuccessful. He told me that if I waited a few minutes I would see a sunbeam streaming through a small window and shining on the roll of honour in the dark interior, and would then be able to photograph the tombstone. A few moments later we took our photographs of the name of Izak Liebenberg and the friendship was struck.

This chance meeting was the beginning of a long association between Abrie Oosthuizen and myself. We corresponded on a regular basis and eventually discovered the grave of Izak Liebenberg in the Philippolis district. My original idea was to write a book for the English-speaking public, but in consultation with Abrie it was decided to first publish in Afrikaans. His idea was very sound as we were both aware of the pending centenary of the outbreak of the Anglo-Boer War. Because of his knowledge of the Cape rebels and his being an Afrikaans historian, I had no hesitation in agreeing to a joint project. All my research documentation and photographs were put at his disposal. Our venture was on.

Over the thousands of graves of the fallen during this awesome conflict a handshake was all that was needed.

GRAHAM JOOSTE
East London
January 1999

Words, Words
In Passing

'To be hanged! Hanged! Hanged!'
Commander Llewellyn

'My God! my God! see and behold these deeds
which are being done to me and my nation.'
Frederik Marais

'My Jesus is now at my side.'
Johannes Coetzee, 16

'And so I now kiss you with my love, and farewell,
farewell, farewell my beloved friend.'
Abraham Jooste

'My wife, my wife, place on my grave,
"Innocent blood! Innocent blood!" '
Hendrik van Heerden

'A person can remain an Afrikaner only once
you have become a child of God.'
Commandant Lötter

'Save your Nation, my God, and let
justice prevail.'
Commandant Scheepers

'He was an ordinary warrior, Lord,
and no rebel.'
DJ Opperman

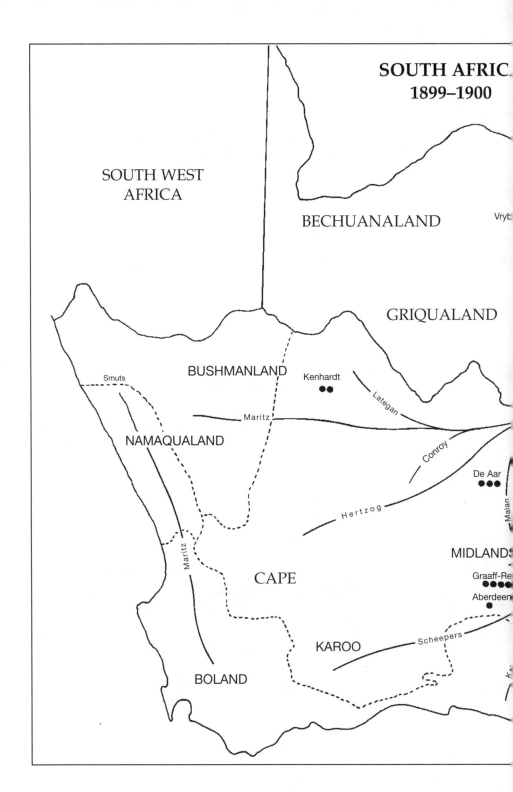

SOUTH AFRIC.
1899–1900

SOUTH WEST
AFRICA

BECHUANALAND

Vryb

GRIQUALAND

BUSHMANLAND

Smuts

Kenhardt

Lategan

Maritz

NAMAQUALAND

Conroy

De Aar

Hertzog

Malan

MIDLAND:

Graaff-Re

Aberdeen

Maritz

CAPE

KAROO

Scheepers

BOLAND

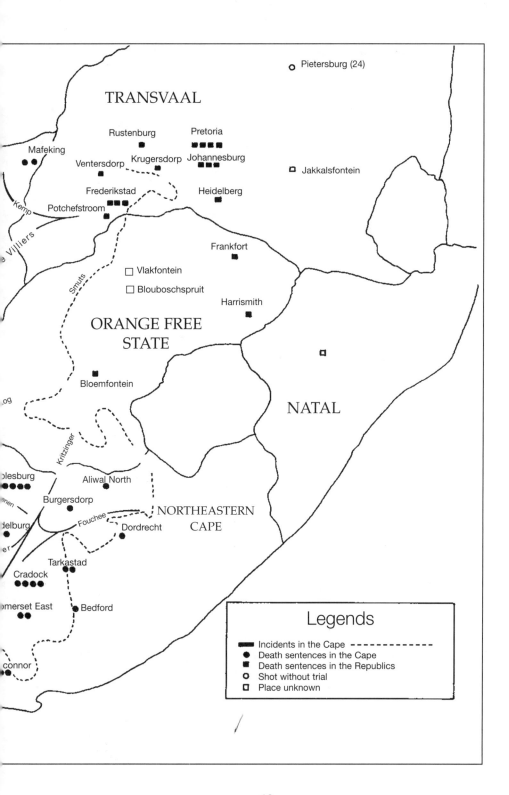

TRANSVAAL

○ Pietersburg (24)

Rustenburg Pretoria
Mafeking
Ventersdorp Krugersdorp Johannesburg
◻ Jakkalsfontein

Frederikstad Heidelberg
Potchefstroom

Frankfort

☐ Vlakfontein
☐ Blouboschspruit
Harrismith

ORANGE FREE
STATE

Bloemfontein

NATAL

lesburg
Aliwal North
Burgersdorp
NORTHEASTERN
delburg Fouchee Dordrecht CAPE

Tarkastad
Cradock

merset East Bedford

connor

Legends

▬▬ Incidents in the Cape --------
● Death sentences in the Cape
■ Death sentences in the Republics
○ Shot without trial
◻ Place unknown

Executions in
the Cape Colony

Many Cape rebels were executed by firing squad. The condemned person was blindfolded and tied to a chair in front of his open grave. Two bags of quicklime lay in readiness on the other side of the grave. The so-called 'undesirables' were forced to witness the execution.
Photograph: War Museum of the Boer Republics

CHAPTER 1

Two Bags of
Unslaked Lime

'No, perhaps he is still lying dead somewhere; but Lord, and the bones, show me, give me the burden of my womb so that I will not be compelled to roam, search and unearth; but eventually to rest in the knowledge that he died from lead and lies under two grain bags of unslaked lime ...'

Prayer for the Bones: DJ Opperman

At least 60 burgers from the Cape Colony and the Republics died before firing squads or on the gallows during the Anglo-Boer War after trials by Military Courts. Others were summarily executed without trial.[1]

How did these men meet their deaths?

Here is a description of the execution of a Cape rebel, found in the book *Hoe Zij Stierven*, followed by the postmortem medical report found in the Archives in Cape Town.[2]

'On the 11th of October he was brought to the marketplace to hear his sentence. The ceremony began with the calling out of certain names which had been listed. Certain "undesirables" had received notices to be present at a specific time. During the roll call they had to answer when their names were called out. If they were not present they faced a jail sentence or a £10 fine.

'Jacobus listened calmly to his sentence which was read out at precisely two o'clock and by one o'clock the next day the sentence would have been carried out. He was then taken back to his cell. He now had twenty-three hours left of his life.

'An English-speaking priest obtained permission to visit him. What was discussed is unknown to us. We did however hear that the witnessing and testimony of Jacobus was so powerful that the priest had no doubt of his deep religious outlook. It is probable that the minister wrote to England regarding the execution, because a letter was received from there asking whether all the condemned men met their death in such a calm manner.

'At the prison were two of his friends who would accompany him to his grave. An inspanned mule-wagon stood ready to carry him there. He left the gaol supported by two soldiers. His arms rested on their shoulders and their arms were wrapped around him. He could not walk without help! Oh! how he has changed! He was pale and done for. What could the reason be? Was it because of his incarceration, or the food he had been given, or an illness, or was he suffering from diarrhoea?

'Pale and weak he was helped onto the wagon which came to a halt next to a trench. He was helped from the wagon, assisted through the trench and taken to his grave about seventy paces on. The soldiers helped him as they had done at the prison. Next to the grave stood a chair. He was assisted onto it. Next to the grave lay two bags of unslaked lime, a watercart and four convicts.

Jacobus Schoeman is tied to a chair outside Tarkastad before being executed.
Source: Hoe Zij Sterven

'Jacobus was tied to the chair and blindfolded with a black cloth. The priest then read a few passages from the Bible and knelt before him in prayer. He then said goodbye and walked away. About twenty-five paces from the grave were twelve armed soldiers. Six were in a kneeling position and six standing behind them. When the sign was given they all fired together. Schoeman's head fell backwards and he died immediately. The doctor undid his shirt and pointed to four bullet-holes in his chest. One shot had gone through his left eye.

'The four convicts untied him, wrapped him in a blanket and lowered him into the grave. The two grainbags of unslaked lime were spread over the body and the outlet from the watercart uncorked. The water poured into the grave. It started to smoke, foam and bubble. The foam was visible above the grave.

'After a while the grave was filled in with soil and so ended the history of Jacobus Schoeman.'

Medical Report
The Commandant,
Tarkastad
14/10/1901

I witnessed the execution of the prisoner Schoeman and did a postmortem examination.

There were seven bullet wounds.

Two punctured the left superior matilla and passed through the base of the skull in the occipital bone to the left of the middle line. Brain substance exuded from each wound of exit.

One wound entering right clavicle passing through the neck and making its exit through the 6th cervical vertebrae.

One wound of entrance in the mid line sternum on a level with the 3rd intercostal space making its exit directly behind through dorsal vertebrae.

One wound of entry through apex of the heart.

One wound of entry above left nipple through heart.

Death was instant.

Signed. Maj. M Brum

This is how Cape Rebels were executed.

CHAPTER 2

Rebels or Ordinary Soldiers?

When reading the inscriptions on the graves or monuments of the executed Boers erected in the Cape Colony, one is moved by the veneration shown by the words:

Hero of the Anglo-Boer War
John Baxter: Aberdeen

Highest toll paid for Nation and Fatherland
Petrus Klopper: Burgersdorp

Greater love hath no man, That he lays down his life for his friends
Willie Louw: Colesberg

... who in the spring of 1901 paid the highest toll
for their love of the Fatherland
Kuhn brothers, Jansen and Rautenbach: Vryburg

Innocent but sentenced to death
Nienaber brothers and Nieuwoudt: Hanover

Heroes to the last drop of blood
Fearless, brave, faithful and good
Piet Bester and other rebels: Dordrecht

He abides in this land now, and for evermore
Gideon Scheepers: Graaff-Reinet

They died so that our freedom could live
Van Onselen and Rittenberg: Kariega

For country and nation you gave your life
Duty, courage and glory never be forgotten
HJ van Heerden: Middelburg

Author's note: The above are translations from the Dutch and Afrikaans inscriptions.

In commemorative albums and history books published during the 1940s, they have each and every one of them been hailed as heroes and martyrs who fought and died for their country.

In recent years various historians have maintained that citizens of the Cape Colony who took up arms against Britain were in fact rebels and were therefore guilty of high treason. The authorities were therefore legally bound to proceed with prosecutions to inhibit further deeds being perpetrated by such persons. Furthermore, they did not have the right to commit deeds that were against the norms of civilized warfare. What then was the Cape rebel; an insurgent or a hero?

A rebel is defined as someone who fights against, resists or refuses allegiance to the established government; a person who resists authority and control; a person who would overthrow a legal power by force. The question now arises; what authority did the Cape rebels try to destabilise or overthrow?

The most elementary observation is one that reads as follows: 'More than 300 Afrikaners were taken into custody by the British authorities in the Cape Colony, tried, and some executed. They were Cape rebels **who rose against the legal government.** In the Transvaal, a rebellion also broke out in 1914 ...'[1]

To compare the so-called rebellion of 1899–1902 to that of the 1914 one in the Transvaal is a major error. While the 1914 revolt took on the form of a popular protest against the legal authorities regarding the annexation of South-West Africa, this was not the case with the activities of the Cape rebels. They did not try to overthrow their legally elected government, but went to the aid of the Republics in their fight for independence. At numerous trials it was made clear that the rebels had nothing against their lawful government, and were in fact loyal subjects. In general the Cape Afrikaners were loyalist-inclined and loved their Queen. Many displayed pictures of her in their homes – proof enough of their loyalty.[2] The historian Amery commented in this regard: 'The Afrikaner is essentially a law-abiding citizen and obedient to the authority of its own creation.'

In his thesis on the Afrikaner in the Cape Colony during the Anglo-Boer War, Snyman also comes to the conclusion that the rebel lion was not about being freed from British rule but simply to assist the Republics in their fight for self-rule. Such an action was certainly not irreconcilable with their loyalty to the Queen.[3] Considering their acceptance of the lawful government, the term 'rebel' was certainly a misnomer.

They did not intrinsically rebel against Britain, as they were satisfied with colonial rule and the freedom that the crown allowed the Cape government.

Despite all these factors they became involved when the Republics took up arms against Britain. The blood and family ties between them were too strong to be overlooked, and because they had a legitimate case against a foreign power, they came to their fellow Afrikaners' aid. By doing so they denied themselves their own freedom in order to restrain England only until the independence of the Republics would once more be recognised.[4]

Because of Britain's scorched-earth policy in the Republics and the stringent martial law regulations imposed upon them, the Cape Afrikaners became uneasy at the thought that these laws might be applied to them as well. This perception gathered momentum around the possibility that the conflict was not purely about the independence of the Republics but the possible extermination of the Afrikaner himself. Boundaries became irrelevant and it was now viewed as a fight for the survival of the Afrikaner.[5] Because of this many condemned rebels stated that they entered the conflict because of the cruelty inflicted upon their people in the Transvaal and Free State and that they had not revolted against their government.[6] In this sense, they were therefore not rebels but brothers-in-arms against a foreign aggressor.

Furthermore the rebels did not take up arms as a large body of men, but more as individuals after certain areas of the Colony in which they resided had been annexed by the Republics. Burgers were commandeered into the invading Boer forces with guaranteed immunity against future reprisals, as they were now burgers of the Republics and could therefore not be classed as rebels.[7]

The Cape rebel was in fact only a rebel because he was a British citizen and the Cape was a British colony. Only in this instance could the charge of high treason be levelled at those who took up arms. The military authorities were therefore within their rights under martial law to prevent the spreading of a rebellion and to neutralise the rebels. It was the right of the state, if not its duty, under martial law to maintain law and order.[8]

Involvement was therefore high treason, and punishable by death, and any of the 10 000 rebels under arms could have been charged with high treason and executed. With regard to the sentencing and execution of a 16-year-old boy rebel who was charged with attempted murder purely on the grounds that he had participated in a skirmish with the enemy, a British newspaper commented: 'His hanging is quite indefensible unless we are resolved to hang all rebels as such.'[9]

Rebels were not only executed for high treason but also for 'barbarous acts contrary to the customs of war' and 'murder'. Other charges included train robbery, arson, plunder, theft and 'disgraceful conduct of a cruel kind', all of which carried the death penalty, thus transgressing the law as well as human rights.[10] These norms, however, did not apply to the British forces during the war, as highlighted by the British newspaper, the *Morning Leader,* after the death sentence had been passed on Gideon Scheepers for various crimes, including arson. It stated: 'It would be too ludicrous to shoot him for indulging in a practice which we were first to introduce into South African warfare.'[11] It is indeed ironical that so many rebels were executed for crimes that fell below the norms of civilised warfare, while it was actually the accuser that stood condemned before the world for its destructive methods against property and population and the complete violation of the Hague Convention.[12] Measured against the norms that were set by Britain, the rebels were not war criminals.

No matter how unfair and unreasonable these norms actually were, the fact remains that by taking up arms as colonials they were justly classified as rebels. 'Although they had a strong moral case, they deserved what they got because no Authority can let rebels go unpunished. It appears that the Cape rebels could count themselves fortunate that a lot more were not executed', wrote Snyman.[13]

Against this unyielding, technically correct attitude, it can be argued that the so-called rebels did not revolt against their own government but went to the aid of their kin who were battling to maintain their rightful independence. They were thus ordinary soldiers who had taken up arms against an aggressor!

A striking attitude is found in DJ Opperman's poem on the execution of Gideon Scheepers, which could also be applied to every burger who was executed for his independence ideals: 'He was an ordinary warrior, Lord, and no rebel.'[14]

The question arises: were the deeds of the Cape rebels legal because they had a legal cause, and can they be honoured as heroes?

No matter how difficult it is to determine right from wrong during a war, the answer is relatively simple: only the winner decides between right and wrong during a conflict and only history determines whether the actors in the drama are called heroes, malcontents, criminals or rebels. Under these circumstances, the cynical conclusion of a historian is fitting: 'A rebellion will only be deemed lawful if it succeeds, and in this case it did not succeed.'[15]

Because they lost the struggle, they were rebels. Had they been the victors, they would have been hailed as heroes.

Forty-four executions were carried out by the British military on burgers in the Cape Colony during the Anglo-Boer War. Their hero status hinges on the interpretation of the individual, and the truth always has two sides. There is, however, a lesson to be learned from this tragic chapter in our history: reconciliation does not revolve around the truth, but purely through forgiveness.

CHAPTER 3

The Military
Courts

When the Transvaal and Free State commandos invaded the Cape Colony in November 1899, about 10 000 colonials either volunteered or were conscripted into their ranks. They were immediately informed that charges of high treason would be inevitable if they were captured, as they would be classified as rebels, not soldiers, and prisoner-of-war status would be denied them. By early 1900 all the Boer commandos had been driven back onto Republican soil and the colonials were granted general amnesty provided they took an oath of neutrality, which included the acknowledgement that they had made themselves liable to be charged with high treason. The majority of Cape rebels accepted this offer but the rest decided to continue fighting within the Transvaal and Free State.

The handling of rebel sentences soon created vexation among the Boers and in October the Cape Parliament passed the Treason Act, giving authority to a Special Court to deal with rebel matters. In future all rebels were to be graded into two categories. The Class I tag would be for all the 'ringleaders' who had fanned the flames of rebellion and who had rank and authority. They would have to appear in court to be tried but the court would not have the power to pass the death sentence. The Class II rebels were of the ordinary rank-and-file burgers who were allowed to return home but could still be brought to trial for offences committed during the war. Within a few months, all the Cape rebel leaders were behind bars, but no death sentences had been imposed.

On 15 December 1900, the Boer commandos once again crossed the

Orange River and this second invasion had far-reaching effects. The guerilla warfare pattern now employed by the Boers was viewed with alarm by the British, who feared a general uprising among the Cape Afrikaners. Martial law was immediately reinstated in all the districts where it had been abolished, and proclaimed in many others. Stricter regulations were imposed on the populace and movement was heavily restricted.

The British military authorities were of the opinion that the Special Court that dealt with rebel matters did not possess enough power to curtail the spreading of rebellion and that most juries had been sympathetic towards the accused. Kitchener's opinion was that swift and forceful methods, as well as heavy sentences, would put an end to any further thoughts of rebellion. The solution would be the appointment of a Military Court with unlimited powers of decision and the authority to pass the death sentence.[1]

On 2 April 1901, the law establishing these military courts was promulgated. The Special Courts retained jurisdiction over serious crimes until that date.

There were specific guidelines laid down for the establishment of the Military Courts, regarding procedures and competence. The court would be presided over by a senior officer who would be assisted by two officers with at least the rank of captain. They had to be experienced in military law judgement. Further assistance from a magistrate would be desirable.

The proceedings of the court would be public and the accused would be entitled to legal representation, the calling of witnesses and the cross-examination of state witnesses. Complete records of all the evidence would be kept. The death sentence could not be carried out without being ratified by Lord Kitchener of Khartoum, General Officer Commanding.

A death sentence had to be the unanimous conclusion of the court and had to be examined by a competent law advisor. Eventually, however, it had to be confirmed by Kitchener. A copy of the procedures was to be forwarded to the Attorney-General in Cape Town who could pass comment on but not revoke the findings of the court.

In practice, these courts paid scant attention to these procedures. According to a directive about martial law, it is aptly defined as follows:

'Martial Law is not a law in the proper sense of the word. It is rather the subordination of the ordinary law to the will of the military commander.' These military courts now had unlimited powers and were only answerable to their commanding officers.[2]

The officers who served in these courts were usually unfamiliar with legal proceedings and unacquainted with the delivery of an unbiased and skilful address. What was law and what was classified as lawful was of little interest to them. It was, therefore, as nothing more than a show for the outside world that these courts were convened. They were merely instruments in the hands of the politicians to put fear into the people.[3]

Where a death sentence was valid for the taking up of arms, many other irrelevant charges appeared on the sheet so as to appease any possible questioning body. To find such charges was obviously not a problem. In practice, 'stealing' and 'marauding' on a charge sheet only referred to horses, donkeys, mules, sheep or fodder commandeered. 'Murder' and 'attempted murder' would mean that the rebel had been armed at the time of conflict and that he could have fired at the British, either wounding, killing or missing them. Being 'active in arms' referred to those who were unsuitable for action or had just joined the commandos as horse-keepers. 'Abusive language,' 'conduct of a cruel nature', 'disgraceful conduct' and 'barbarous acts contrary to the customs of war' were terms used in charges against those who were sentenced to death. It was simply to find the stick that would beat the dog.[4]

Rebels known as 'persons of standing' within their community or leaders in a commando were without exception sentenced to death and executed. This was a system applied to ensure that the top structures of Boer society, as well as the commandos, would be destroyed.

This saw the beginning of a string of gruesome executions throughout the Cape Colony. Practically every district wherein the guerilla commandos operated had its turn to witness an execution. To ensure that the executions would have the maximum effect as a deterrent upon the people, General French ordered that they be carried out in public.

In addition, it was decreed that all persons under suspicion of being sympathetic towards the Boers were compelled to attend the public executions of rebels. They became known as the 'undesirables' and included teachers, ministers, deacons and church elders, who formed the backbone of Afrikaner society. If there was not enough evidence available to prosecute and incarcerate these leaders, they were rounded up and sent to Port Alfred without trial for the duration of the war. Executions became festive spectacles. The condemned had to appear before a full military parade to hear their sentences read out. Attendance

Some of the more than 200 undesirables detained in the internment camp at Port Alfred.
The Rev. Radloff is seated in the second row, fourth from the left.
Photograph: Gevangenis-Stemme *1903, by the Rev. CH Radloff*

'Undesirables' are gathered on a village square to attend an execution.
Photograph: War Museum of the Boer Republics

by the populace was compulsory and places of business and schools had to close. Military bands were in attendance, as well as detachments from the Town Guards and other colonial regiments. In Graaff-Reinet, the Coldstream Guards band struck up the tune *More work for the undertaker* after an execution.[5]

The commandant of the occupying forces usually read out the sentence in a loud, commanding voice for all to hear. On one occasion a commandant bellowed: 'To be hanged! Hanged! Hanged!'[6]

As can be seen from court records, the customary method of execution was hanging. However, because of the cumbersome structure of gallows and the problem of transportation from town to town, as well as the timing of the arrival of the executioner, it was decided to make use of firing squads. By now each town had been occupied by the British forces and the garrisons could supply the firing squads. The majority of the executed died in this fashion. In one town, a windmill was used as a gallows when it was discovered that it did not have one.

The pro-British press was delighted with the establishment of the Military Courts and the heavy sentences they imposed. They were of the opinion that the rebels had been treated too lightly and that the measure of removing their franchise would not discourage them in any way. In a sense, they were correct as many rebels did not have the right to vote because: 'They belong to the so-called poor white and *bywoner* class.'[7]

Among the first rebels to be hanged was a 16-year-old boy and a retarded horse guard who looked after the horses. Shortly after this public hanging, the Aliwal North *Northern Post* commented, on 17 July 1901: 'With reference to the hanging of rebels the general opinion appears to be that it will effectively prevent the spread of rebellion. The British loyalists are jubilant.'[8]

The injury to the Afrikaners resulting from these executions was only surpassed by the suffering endured by the women and children in the concentration camps.

CHAPTER 4

Illegal Executions

In their eagerness to please the military authorities the Military Courts had the audacity to charge and try non-combatents. Some received prison terms while others received the death sentence even before these laws became statute. Four burgers were executed early in March 1901 while the official installations of Military Courts was only recognised on 12 April. Though the Attorney-General ruled that the cases were illegal, it was too late. No retrial could be held as the executions had already taken place.

Hendrik Jacobus van Heerden (34)
Executed on 2 March 1901 on the farm Zevenfontein,
Middelburg district.[1]

This respected farmer and shopkeeper was the first to face the firing squad of the occupying British forces. It was one of the most shameful and barbaric miscarriages of justice and neglect of duty by the British authorities imaginable. Was this act to be an indication of the bitter days that lay ahead?

Van Heerden, in fact, was not a rebel at all. He was a moderate, middle-aged, loyal British subject. On 1 March 1901, a commando of Commandant Kritzinger passed by and obtained fresh horses and provisions. Shortly after they left, a group of Colonel Gorringe's mounted column arrived who were shadowing the Boer commando. They immediately arrested Van Heerden for questioning in Middelburg.

He saddled up and joined the British column. They were about 200 yards from his shop and house when a volley of gunfire struck them from a small hill close to the road. Van Heerden was badly wounded, fell from his horse and staggered toward the hill, waving his arms and indicating that the firing should cease. Two troopers received slight wounds. Van Heerden's wife and servant managed to get him to the house. Later in the afternoon an ambulance arrived to fetch the British wounded. Van Heerden received constant attention from his wife. The important question here was: did the Boers know Van Heerden was in the column or was he leading his captors into an ambush? The Attorney-General was eventually of the opinion that Van Heerden was unaware of the presence of the Boers on the hill, because he was the first to be struck down by gunfire. The irregular Military Court, however, judged that it was treachery.

Hendrik van Heerden of Sewefontein, Middelburg. Source: Hoe Zij Sterven

A day after the incident a column of soldiers arrived. The lieutenant in charge kicked open the bedroom door and informed the wounded Van Heerden that he had been tried by a competent court and had been found guilty of treason. Furthermore, he stated that Van Heerden had exactly eight minutes in which to prepare himself. According to reports, it appears Colonel Gorringe held court on the adjoining farm, Rietvlei. All the witnesses were African labourers and on their evidence he was sentenced to death *in absentia*. Gorringe later stated that, due to lack of time, he could not refer this case to a higher authority and it was imperative to conclude it as soon as possible.[2]

Van Heerden, who was in great pain, was pulled from his wife by soldiers, lifted on his blanket and carried outside. There was a volley of shots from behind the kraal wall, then silence. Minutes later the executioners arrived back in the house and dumped the dying Van Heerden back onto his bed. He died in his wife's arms.

There appears to be no doubt that this was to serve as an example to future 'would-be-rebels'. It however is very evident that the Military

Court had no jurisdiction over this case. Secondly, according to Military Court procedures, the accused had to be present at his hearing. Legal representation was an essential factor as well. Thirdly, all sentences had to be ratified by higher authorities, but here was a case of the officer in charge ratifying the sentence himself. Also to take into consideration was the fact that Van Heerden could not defend the allegations brought against him by the African witnesses. The most absurd thing was that he was executed as an ordinary prisoner.

The magistrate later stated to the Cape law department: 'It seems almost incredible that a wounded prisoner could, under any circumstances, be executed by a British Officer.'[3] The Attorney-General stated: 'I need hardly point out that even in the case of a military tribunal, a trial in the absence of the accused is no trial at all.'[4]

After a ministerial investigation, the case was referred to Kitchener, who ratified his execution. He stated that he had received faulty reports and there were time delays. Furthermore, he maintained that no further investigation was necessary and the case was closed. It is evident that Kitchener was not concerned about the merits of this tragic incident and he had no interest in it.[5]

The execution of a prisoner without proper trial went against one of the highest principles of the Hague Convention's rules applying to civilised methods of warfare.

Van Heerden's last words to his wife were: 'My wife, my wife, put on my grave, "Innocent blood! Innocent blood".'

Hendrik Jacobus van Heerden was executed on the farm Zevenfontein in the Middelburg district on 2 March 1901. His grave lies next to the road opposite his house and shop. His name appears on the Burger Monument in Middelburg.

Charel Gerhardus Johannes Nienaber (36)
Jan Petrus Nienaber (24)
Johannes (Jan) Andries Nieuwoudt (23)
Executed by firing squad on 19 March 1901 at De Aar.[6]

What exactly happened on that pitch-black night of 18 February 1901 will never be known with certainty. General Wynand Malan and 25 commando members derailed a train near Taaibosch siding near

The grave of Hendrik Van Heerden at Sewefontein, Middelburg.
Photograph: Graham Jooste

Hanover, killing the stoker, two soldiers and two black labourers. Three young men were accused of high treason, murder and robbery and were executed. Two others received heavy sentences. On the monument in the Hanover cemetery, the words 'Innocent and sentenced to death' are to be found.

This incident took place shortly after Malan crossed into the Cape Colony with the purpose of derailing military trains and thus disrupting communications. The night of this particular derailment was dark and foreboding. Heavy rain was falling and visibility was down to less than a yard. Yet three men were sentenced to death on the evidence of one of their friends and some labourers.

Charel and Petrus Nienaber and Jan Nieuwoudt were from the farm De Bad in the Hanover district where they were employed by Andries Pienaar, the owner. They were not on commando. The day after the derailment they were arrested by a British patrol and appeared in court at De Aar. They were charged with having been part of a group that had attacked a military train, killing two soldiers and robbing persons. While they were in custody, one of the detained, Jan van den Berg, turned Crown evidence. His testimony became the focal point of a conviction. According to evidence in court, a small group of commandos approached the accused on 18 February and persuaded them to take part in the derailment at Taaibosch. During the night they were supplied with horses and joined the group. The train was derailed by tearing up part of the line. Upon derailment, the train was fired upon and return fire from the train was encountered by the Boers. After the shooting ceased some black labourers were robbed of their money, according to some witnesses.

The stoker, two soldiers and two black labourers were killed in the incident. The witnesses displayed great uncertainty about who was present, and not because of the bad visibility. One of the black witnesses

Petrus Nienaber of De Bad, Hanover.
Source: Hoe Zij Sterven

Jan Nieuwoudt of De Bad, Hanover.
Source: Hoe Zij Sterven

stated that he recognised Charel Nienaber when the accused struck a match! Because of the evidence given by Van den Berg and the black soldiers, all three were sentenced to death. A fourth burger, who also got the death sentence, received clemency in the form of a five-year jail sentence, while the fifth accused was given a five-year term. Van den Berg, as a Crown witness, was acquitted, but later accused of perjury.

After the death sentences were confirmed by Kitchener, Nieuwoudt and the Nienaber brothers were executed by firing squad at De Aar. They all maintained that Van den Berg had given false evidence to save himself, as they were never at the scene. Nieuwoudt told his father that he forgave Van den Berg because he did not know what he was doing.

The Cape law department was in agreement as to the outcome of this case. They had no hesitation in agreeing that the accused were guilty. Their legal advisor was of the opinion that the accused were ordinary train robbers and murderers, and that they were not part of General Malan's organised attack. However, the law department did acknowledge that the court procedure regarding documentation was questionable and that the sentences were invalid because they were under the jurisdiction of the Special Court. It was however too late, as the sentences had already been carried out.

A year after peace was declared, this trial had an unusual outcome when Petrus Pienaar, the brother of Andries Pienaar of De Bad, laid down his arms at Cradock. A member of Commandant Fouchee's commando, he was arrested and accused of being an accomplice in the derailment at Taaibosch. During his trial, it became clear that Van den Berg had given false evidence about the three who had already paid the supreme penalty. He was arrested and charged with perjury.

The trial took place in Grahamstown. Again the witnesses contradicted each other as to who was present at the scene. General Malan, who had organised the ambush, swore under oath that there were no strange burgers with his commando that night. He also stated that he had never seen the executed men, nor Jan van den Berg. However the black witnesses insisted that they had correctly pointed out the brothers Nienaber and Nieuwoudt at the identification parade in De Aar. This despite the fact that it was so dark that a match had to be struck to see a face!

In the end, the court ruled in favour of Van den Berg, after much deliberation. The charge of perjury was withdrawn and the curtain lowered over this unsavoury case. No truths had been established and there was plenty of bitterness around.

The executions of these three burgers, mainly on the evidence of blacks and black soldiers under British arms, led to some brutal reprisals by the Boer forces against blacks in uniform.[7]

The Boer population was convinced that the three men were innocent, and the inscription on their monument in their hometown, Hanover, bears this sentiment: 'Innocently condemned to death by a Military Court,' and below that, 'I behold the vengeance; I shall repay, sayeth the Lord.'

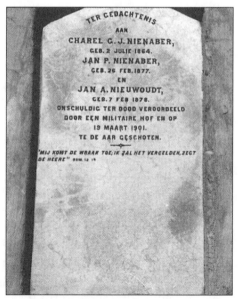

The memorial plaque erected for the Nienaber brothers and Nieuwoudt in the cemetery at Hanover. Photograph: Graham Jooste

35

CHAPTER 5

Hanged in Public

The gruesome manner in which the first three rebels were hanged after being found guilty by Military Courts was a clear message to the populace that no mercy would be shown to rebels. The order for the hangings to be held in public, as well as compulsory presence of the citizenry, was issued by General French himself. It was clear that his intention was to spread fear among the people of the Cape Colony.

During the middle of the 1901 winter, Commandant PH Kritzinger launched an offensive in the northeastern Cape. After his occupation of Jamestown, strong British forces compelled him to withdraw into the Drakensberg mountains. He established camps in the ravines of the Karringmelk River on the farm Wildefontein. Colonel Harry Scobell was assigned the task of dealing with this new threat and was soon on Kritzinger's trail. He was experienced in this type of warfare and had pursued rebels before.

Kritzinger made the fatal mistake of staying four days in the same place and not detailing sufficient pickets to warn against danger. Furthermore, it gave a local farmer enough time to advise Scobell where the Boers were to be found. During the night of 6 June 1901, Scobell's flying column surprised and captured the Boer camp. In the close conflict, at times hand to hand, two British soldiers were wounded and some Boers taken prisoner. While seven of the captured burgers were banished to Bermuda, three were compelled to stand trial at Dordrecht. The charge was to be attempted murder. This was a clear warning to the region described by Milner as 'an awful state, just reeking with treason' during an earlier visit to the area.

The reasons why these three were chosen and the manner in which they were executed caused dismay everywhere, including in Britain.[1] One was a 16-year-old youngster, another a retarded horse guard and the third a respected farmer.

Cornelius Johannes Claassen (22)
Hanged at Somerset East on 24 July 1901.[3]

Claassen, Coetzee and Marais were tried by Military Court at Dordrecht on 24 June 1901. The charge against the three was attempted murder.

Claassen lived with his parents on the farm Bouwersfontein in the Darlington district of the Cape Colony. He was of the labourer class and his parents enjoyed the privilege of staying on the owner's farm, but under certain conditions. He joined the commando of Commandant PH Kritzinger in the Cape Midlands as a horse guard. He was described as heavily built, over six feet tall and retarded.

It was alleged at his trial that he had been one of the burgers who fired upon the British from a hillock during the taking of the Boer position on Wildefontein. It was claimed that when the British stormed the hillock, Gibbons of the CMR was wounded. No witness was called to testify that Claassen had in fact inflicted the wound, but he was however with the men captured on the hillock.

Claassen pleaded guilty to high treason because he was on commando, but emphatically denied having fired a shot, as his work was to look after the horses. He was nevertheless found guilty and given the death sentence, which was ratified by Kitchener on 12 July.

Claassen was interned in the Dordrecht gaol for a month, entirely unaware of his death sentence. He was transported to his home town of Somerset East for his execution. The gallows were ready and the hangman had arrived.

On 23 July, the inhabitants of Somerset East were summoned to gather at the market square to hear the proclamation of sentence passed on Cornelius Claassen. About 1000 people were in attendance, under the strict control of the Royal Fusileers, Town Guards and various colonial detachments. The prisoners from the gaol were transported on an ox-wagon to bear witness to the unfolding event. Moments later the accused arrived on a cart escorted by a detachment of troops. Claassen was brought before Commandant Llewellyn who had climbed onto a wagon to announce his fate. Llewellyn read the proclamation and a bellowing voice ended:

'To be hanged! Hanged! Hanged!'

Claassen listened to the proceedings with his head bowed, but it seemed as if he did not grasp what was going on around him, and the pastor of the Dutch Reformed Church was compelled to translate for him. After this the silent crowd drifted away and Claassen was taken back to his cell. The Reverend JH Hofmeyer of Cookhouse and the Venerable Reverend Oates took it in turns to console and support the accused through the night. During that evening all the so-called 'undesirables' received notices to attend the hanging at the gaol the following morning. These were all the leaders of the Afrikaner community, including churchmen, teachers and prominent citizens. Ramsay MacDonald, the outspoken English Member of Parliament, later had good reason to speak out that martial law in the Cape Colony was indeed a law against the Afrikaner.[4]

Reverend Hofmeyer accompanied Claassen to the scaffold. The accused walked with firm steps towards the scaffold and climbed the narrow stairs unaided. A white hood was placed over his head, his legs bound with rope and the noose put around his neck. The gathered citizens were compelled to watch and those who turned their heads away had them wrenched back by the guards. A young man who pulled his hat over his eyes had it knocked off and was warned to watch what happened to rebels.

The last resting place of Cornelius Johannes Claassen is unknown. The only existing memory of him is in the Somerset East museum, where a walking stick with his name carved upon it by a burger interned in the Port Alfred camp is kept.

Johannes Petrus Coetzee (16)
Hanged at Cradock on 13 July 1901.[5]

This 16-year-old boy from Paardekraal in the Cradock district was captured with Claassen and Marais at Wildefontein and brought to court in Dordrecht on 24 June 1901. The charges against him were high treason and the attempted murder of a soldier called Gibbons. Johannes

Petrus Coetzee of Paardekraal, Cradock.

Source: Hoe Zij Sterven

acknowledged that he had joined the Boer commando but denied the attempted murder charge. He was found guilty by the Military Court and sentenced to death.

Coetzee was held in the Dordrecht gaol until four days before his execution in his home town, Cradock, unaware of his impending death.

The British commandant of Cradock issued an order that all male members of the population had to gather on the Dutch Reformed Church square at 11 am on 12 July for the proclamation of the death sentence. All businesses and schools were ordered to close for the ceremony. The beautiful church was occupied by the military and sandbags were placed so as to close off all the windows. Armed troops covered the roof. A platform was erected on the church square and both infantry and cavalry formed up in readiness to deal with any disturbances.

A large crowd had gathered as Coetzee was brought before the town commandant. He heard his death sentence in bewilderment and, while still confused, was led away to his cell. He was to die the following day on the gallows erected at the gaol. It was evident that the boy had not expected the sentence meted out to him.

He was visited in his cell by a minister of the church to prepare him to face his ordeal. The minister counselled him to ask the Lord's forgiveness for his sins. The youngster stated that his conscience was clear and that he had murdered no one. He had joined the Transvaal commando to help in the fight against his oppressed nation and if he had to die for that, then he was prepared to do so. These words spoken by a 16-year-old boy were one of the main reasons why so many Boers chose the rebel road. When young Petrus, as he was known, was visited by his father the following morning he was calm, and greeted his father with these words: 'Father, please tell Mother and our family that they must not mourn for me. I am fine. I am going to my Saviour and to my blessed eternal home. I know you will all mourn for me and that is what is tormenting me.'

Sixteen-year-old Petrus Coetzee (in the centre between the two warders and wearing a hat)
listens to his death sentence on the church square in Cradock.
Source: After Pretoria, *by Wilson*

A few minutes later the executioner arrived and tied his hands. He was led to the backyard of the prison where a large number of 'undesirables' had been forced to gather, among them some burgers who were out on parole or bail. A roll-call was taken to ensure that all were in attendance.

Reverend JC Reyneke of the Dutch Reformed Church accompanied him onto the scaffold, reading these comforting words: 'I am the resurrection and the life. Whoever believes in me will have life even unto death.' Moments before the trapdoor was sprung, Coetzee was heard to utter: 'My Jesus is now at my side.'

His elderly father was not allowed to claim the body, which was placed on a scotch-cart drawn by four convicts and taken to a grave somewhere along the banks of the Fish River, outside the town. The authorities did, however, allow his father and the Reverend Reyneke to accompany the burial cart. During the proceedings, the faithful gathered in silent prayer at their churches. A black flag fluttered in the breeze above the prison.

At the conclusion of the proceedings, Reyneke and the community leaders were summoned to the town commandant's office. He informed them that 'the blood of Coetzee will be claimed from you and all the other Dutch ministers'.

According to the British newspaper, *Morning Leader*, the trial and conviction of Coetzee was highly questionable. It reported that: 'The court had only the most elementary notions of evidence. There was obviously no adequate evidence on which to convict him. He was a very young man, neither ruffian nor brigand and certainly in no sense a ringleader. His hanging was quite indefensible unless we are resolved to hang all rebels as such.'[6]

A leading English parliamentarian warned: 'One great act of injustice, one execution of an innocent man, will for generations be embedded in the minds of a nation. The execution of Coetzee could well lead to another Slagtersnek!'[7] The name of Johannes Coetzee is to be found on the Burger Monument in the garden of the Dutch Reformed Church in Cradock, but his grave is unknown.

Frederick Abram Marais (32)
Hanged at Middelburg on 10 July 1901.[8]

Marais was a married man with small children who farmed at Langkloof in the Middelburg district. He was captured with Claassen and Coetzee at Wildefontein on the night of 6 June 1901 and stood trial in Dordrecht. He was incarcerated in the town and taken to Middelburg on 9 July for his execution.

On that day, the population was compelled to attend the proclamation of sentence, which was to be carried out on the market square. Asked if he had anything to say in mitigation of sentence, he referred to the oppressive martial law and added: 'The English interned many of our people who had done nothing wrong! That is why I joined the Boer forces. I have nothing more to say.' [9]

A shocked Marais then heard for the first time that he was to be hanged the following day. Reeling from the news of his impending death, he was escorted under guard to his cell. Before his execution, he wrote a stirring letter to his wife Annie and his children.

Frederik Abram Marais.
Photograph made available by
DJ Marais of Bronkhorstspruit

Middelburg, 8 July 1901

Dear and never forgotten Wife,

Herewith I must bring you the sad tidings that I have to leave you. But, my beloved, do not be troubled and mourn over it, because it is the will of God. If it was not His will then I would have escaped it. But, oh, think of Hendrik van Heerden. I must follow him. You must do your best never to forget the Lord.

You must not suspect me of such, because our dearest God and Lord Jesus said: 'Your thoughts are not My thoughts and your adversity is not My adversity.' Therefore, my dearest, be satisfied and do not complain about it. I must just depart a short while before you.

My love, never forget how we prayed in the evenings on our knees praising and trusting in Him. Raise our children up in the Lord. Oh! that we could meet again in heaven where there is no anguish and tears and none of us will be missing. Oh! that we will all be at the right hand of God.

Dearest wife, you must be contented. Ask the Lord to be your rod and staff in the difficult days to follow. Go quietly to one side and ask the Lord for help. He is constantly willing to help. Oh! I never thought that I could bear this, but my loving Jesus gives me my strength to carry on.

By the blessing of the Lord I have the minister of Middelburg with me. Because of his conversations with me I enjoyed a restful night. Furthermore, my loved one, now be satisfied. You know where we shall meet again. So I say, 'until we meet again! Until we meet again!'

Oh, my darling Annie and my children, I command you all to the hand of the Lord. He will help. Now I do not know what to write about any further. My time is now so short and precious. I ask you to visit your brother Fanie, he should again keep Frekie with him. You can therefore do something for him. If you can, give him twenty ewes and let him go to his father.

Dearest one, I do not know what to tell you; whether you should go to Grandpa, but I place you in the hands of brother Martinus after the death of Grandpa. He must think about how much we loved each other and still do. Please give this letter to Mother and Grandpa to read as well as my brothers and sisters.

Oh! my parents, brothers and sisters, always do your best to keep the loving Lord before your eyes, never forsake him. Oh, will it not be glorious for all of us to meet up there, where we can sing the hymn 'Holy, holy, holy, is the Lord of hosts, peace on earth and peace in the Highest Heavens.'

Brother Fanie, I am no more a person of this earth. Within a short while I must pass along. My brother there is now nothing wrong between us anymore. Everything is right. Look after Annie and my children for as long as you can. Oh, my brother, the Lord will reward you for this. Look after her affairs.

I must now end with best wishes to you my beloved wife and children. I give you all into the hands of the Lord. Best wishes also to Grandpa and Mother as well as to all my brothers and sisters and friends.

I also greet you with greetings from a loved one. Until we meet again, until we meet again, all those that are loved and dear to me.

Your most loving,
FA Marais

Once again a large group of people were ordered to attend the execution and gathered around the scaffold at the prison. Before Marais ascended the gallows steps, he turned to the commandant and officers and said:

The memorial pillar erected in the Middelburg cemetery for Frederik Marais, Petrus Wolfaardt and Commandant Lötter.
Photograph: Rodney Constantine

'As an innocent I am being hanged. I have received the grace to forgive you, but I pray that God will forgive you as well!'

Once on the scaffold, he called out in a strong voice: 'My God! my God! See and behold these deeds that they are doing to me and my nation!'

When the trapdoor opened, he was no more. A hurried inspection of his body certified that he had died by hanging. His family's request for the body was refused. The corpse was taken to a grave in the location for burial. Two bags of lime were poured over the body before it was covered. A week after his execution, his wife was advised of his death.

In 1907, the remains of Marais, together with those of Commandant Lötter and Pieter Wolfaardt, were exhumed and reburied in a communal grave in the cemetery at Middelburg. A monument in their honour was erected and his name also appears on the Burger Monument to the Boer fallen on the town square.

Many more of these gruesome public executions were to follow.

CHAPTER 6

Burgersdorp,
That 'Rebel Nest'

Another shocking public hanging took place in Burgersdorp. The British regarded Burgersdorp as the rebel nest of the Cape Colony,[1] largely because the theological seminary of the Dutch Reformed Church was situated in the town. The principal was the renowned Professor Lion-Cachet of Afrikaans language fame, his students fiery supporters of the Boer republics. In 1893 a monument was erected in acknowledgement of Dutch being made the official language of the Cape Parliament after English.

When the war broke out, nearly all the students broke off their studies and took up arms against the British. Lion-Cachet fell foul of the authorities as a result of his holding church services in the Stormberg for the occupying commandos. After the resounding Boer victory, the retreating British vandalised the Language Monument and removed it to an unknown place. Upon the reoccupation of Burgersdorp by the British, Lion-Cachet was thrown into prison. The capture of young Petrus Klopper and his subsequent treatment by the military offered the opportunity to give this area a warning.

Petrus Willem Klopper(t) (20)
Hanged at Burgersdorp on 20 July 1901.[2]

Klopper, from the farm Kleinfontein in the Burgersdorp district, surrendered to the British forces who had occupied the town, having joined Commandant GHP van Reenen when he entered the Cape with his commando, his reason being the brutality towards the women and children of the Free State by the military.

He had been on commando for only three days when he was captured in a farmhouse at Ruigtevlei with two others on the night of 7 June. This skirmish in the Steynsburg district resulted in the capture of nine Boers, including the young Klopper. According to witnesses, the British patrol stormed the house and demanded immediate surrender. Shots were fired from outside the house, resulting in the death of two troopers. During this period, Klopper was asleep in the house and was awakened by the British entry and subsequent rifle fire. Witnesses stated that Klopper did not fire a single shot as the action occurred outside the house and Klopper immediately surrendered. The British officers could not confirm that the young man was responsible for the deaths of the soldiers.

One of the captured Boers managed to escape but the rest were taken prisoner. It appears that Klopper was singled out because he had broken his oath of neutrality after previously laying down his arms.

The trial commenced at Steynsburg and Klopper pleaded guilty to treason but not guilty to murder. On 17 June he was found guilty on all charges and removed to the Burgersdorp gaol to await his fate, and a month later the sentence of death was ratified. During his incarceration, he became aware that he was to be hanged only because of the erection of gallows within the confines of the walled prison. For days he heard the knocking and sawing of the construction gang outside his cell door.

The inhabitants of Burgersdorp were ordered to be present for the reading of sentence on the town square. All Afrikaner community leaders had to answer a roll-call. The proclamation of sentence was made under an old bluegum tree, the stump of which is still to be seen today, and has become a monument. Here Petrus Klopper heard that he was to be executed by hanging on the following day.

Back in his cell, people heard him singing loudly from Psalm 146 and later falling into prayer. Attorney Hofmeyer drew up the youngster's will and he was visited by Lion-Cachet and the Reverend Geyer. Klopper vowed that he was firm in his religion and prepared to die for his nation. Later that evening his parents visited him and he appeared very calm. He read a passage from the scriptures for them. He then wrote his name in the Bible and handed it over to them. The British

Petrus Klopper(t) (second from left) at the old prison in Burgersdorp just before he was hanged. The 'undesirables' forced to attend the execution are standing in front of the prison. Source: Cultural History Museum, Burgersdorp

guard in charge shed tears and turned his head away. When they all had to leave, the guard offered Petrus a firm handshake with the words: 'God bless you.'

The professors Du Plessis and Snyman spent the rest of the night with him, offering support. When asked if he would like to sleep, he answered: 'Oh no, I want to be awake with my Saviour until the end. If I go to sleep, the enemy will take the opportunity to frighten me.' When he was told that the Boers wanted to avenge him, he became very upset and pleaded for them not to. He cried that vengeance belonged to God alone.

At nine the following morning, the executioner entered his cell and found him praying. The executioner tied his hands and led him to the noose. Prominent local Afrikaners were compelled to witness the execution as a warning. Soldiers were placed on alert around the prison and a guard with fixed bayonets was stationed close to the scaffold.

Klopper climbed the steps firmly as his executioner asked him for forgiveness for the ghastly deed he was about to perform, reassuring him with the words: 'I forgive everybody, as God has forgiven me!'

J Henning of Janspoort was one of those summoned to attend the execution. He had to bring with him all his sons over the age of 16. Years later he recalled the execution.[3]

'When he ascended the steps towards the noose Professor Lion-Cachet called out in a loud voice, "Mercy, O God!" Petrus stood very still with his eyes fixed on us. He appeared very bleak and dismayed.

There were no tears and we could see his eyes still staring at us. When the executioner pulled the cap over his eyes they disappeared forever. When the trap was sprung we saw the rope with its heavy burden swaying back and forth.'

Klopper was buried a short distance outside the town along the Aliwal North road, in the Hottentot murderers' cemetery,[4] and later reburied in a mass grave of Boers who died in the regions of Burgersdorp and the Stormsberg during the war. A tombstone with the names of the fallen in the Burgersdorp cemetery bears witness to their last resting place. His name also appears on the Burger Monument at Burger Square.

The executions of Coetzee, Marais, Claassen and Klopper sent a shock wave through the cemetery.[5] Member of Parliament MJ Pretorius, who was compelled to witness the execution of Marais, protested strongly in Parliament, detailing the barbaric way in which the case was handled. He was instrumental in having a special committee formed to investigate the public executions, which sent a strongly worded message of protest to the governor of the Cape. During their investigations it came to light that the executions were ordered by none other than General French, who was also responsible for the compulsory attendance by members of the public. Kitchener was urged to stop these types of execution immediately.

The reaction of the English-language press was immediate.[6] The *South African News* thundered: 'These Khaki fools are sowing a rich harvest to be reaped by us who remain in the country when they are safe at home.' The *Morning Leader* indicated that there had been a complete miscarriage of justice in the case of Coetzee, arguing that although Coetzee was captured under arms he should not have been tried for murder.

In London, Parliament erupted in fierce debate. It was pointed out in the House that these executions would harden the rebels and not scare them off. The Colonial Secretary contacted Kitchener immediately with a request to halt the executions forthwith.

This request fell on deaf ears. Kitchener was in favour of public executions, claiming that if they were not continued the Boers would find reason to believe that condemned persons would be quietly done away with.[7] In October 1901, four condemned Boers from Vryburg met their end on the gallows made from a windmill! And so the public executions continued. In December of the same year, two Boers were hanged before a crowd of blacks. A Boer was executed by firing squad at Tarkastad before a group of taunting coloured people. As late as 25 January another Boer met his fate in public at Somerset East. If an execution was held in private, then all the internees in the prison were compelled to attend. These executions were later described as: 'unique in the history of civilised nations!'[8]

The memorial stone for the fallen citizens of Burgersdorp. The name of Petrus Klopper(t) of Kleinfontein, Burgersdorp, appears at the top of the list.
Photograph: Abrie Oosthuizen

CHAPTER 7

'In the Sand
of Graaff-Reinet ...'

The Cape Midlands was the heartland of the uprising. Many Boers from the Slagtersnek area joined the Great Trek northwards to be free from British rule. The Boer commandos in the midlands waged guerilla warfare in the hope of sparking off an uprising by the population against the British. The mountain ranges of the Camdeboo, Tandjiesberge, Sneeuberge and the Suurberge offered ideal concealment to the marauding bands of Free State commandos. Their numbers were soon swollen by boys leaving their classrooms as well as farmers and their followers, until the commandos of Scheepers, Lötter, Fouchee, Lategan and Malan consisted almost entirely of Cape rebels. General Smuts always hoped that a mighty uprising by the Afrikaners in the Cape would take root in this area.

Graaff-Reinet, the main town of the area, is situated on the sandy banks of the Sundays River. Most of the skirmishes with British columns occurred a day's ride from this, the heart of the region. Graaff-Reinet not only became the centre of occupation by the British military but also of the suffering to follow.

By the middle of 1901 Graaff-Reinet had become the headquarters of the Military Court with jurisdiction covering the entire eastern section of the Cape. A hundred and sixty rebels were sentenced by this court to banishment across the sea or to death. Many death sentences were passed by this court and those who received reprieves from Kitchener were usually deported to St Helena, Bermuda, Ceylon or India. A total of 18 death sentences were imposed in Graaff-Reinet. The population

Nine rebels being sentenced on the church square of Graaff-Reinet.
Source: After Pretoria, *by Wilson*

had to endure eight of these, and when the inhabitants could endure no more suffering the executions were transferred to surrounding towns to act as warnings.[1]

The stone prison in Graaff-Reinet overflowed not only with rebels but also with 'undesirables'. These were Boers who had transgressed martial law and had to witness the executions. Photographs of Boers awaiting trial in Graaff-Reinet bear witness to this episode. Many were wounded and should have been in hospital. The faces of the men bear silent witness to their sufferings.

While the prisons were overflowing and the firing squads went to work in Graaff-Reinet, Cradock, Middelburg, Tarkastad, Colesberg, Aberdeen, Somerset East, De Aar, Burgersdorp, Aliwal North and Kenhardt, the Republican dream began to evaporate like the smoke from the rifles.

The hope of a large Afrikaner insurrection in the Cape faded, and it was left to a few 'bitter-enders' to continue the struggle. In July 1901 the flying columns of General French commanded by Lieutenant-Colonel Doran were handed over to the command of Colonel Harry Scobell. This energetic and famed rebel hunter was to be responsible for the capture of hundreds of Boer rebels. His prey included the likes of commandants Scheepers, Lötter, Breed and Wolfaardt and lieutenants Liebenberg,

A group of rebels in the prison at Graaff-Reinet. Seven of them died before a firing squad. They are: Daniël Olwagen (2), Frederik Toy (4), Lodewyk Pfeiffer (5), Johan van Rensburg (6), Ignatius Nel (8), Hendrik Veenstra (15) and Petrus Fourie (20). All rebels were photographed once they had been captured. These photogrpahs show clearly that they were in poor physical condition. Source: Graaff-Reinet Museum

Bester and Schoeman. More than half of the total executed were captured by him.

His first big success came on 12 July when he cornered the Scheepers commando in the Camdeboo near Graaff-Reinet.[2] His columns kept on the trail of Scheepers for days on end, but the wily Boers always managed to elude him, on occasions covering up to 50 miles a day. For long spells they were without food and water, having to abandon their pack mules.

After spending a miserable day in the saddle without food and water Scobell camped high up in the Camdeboo. Early the following morning he trapped Scheepers in a kloof on the farm Onbedacht. During the skirmish 35 Boers were captured, among them 27 Cape rebels. Only one British soldier was killed.[3] Much to Scobell's dismay, Scheepers escaped with a large section of his commando. However, he succeeded in capturing one of the commando's most prominent lieutenants, Izak Liebenberg.

The captured Free Staters were banished as prisoners of war while the Cape rebels were charged with high treason. Nine would be executed for crimes ranging from high treason, murder, attempted murder and arson to robbery. Five were to face the firing squad at

Graaff-Reinet, three in Colesberg and one met his death on the gallows in Aliwal North. A few months after the executions, Scheepers, suffering from an acute bout of illness, was captured near Prince Albert. He was later executed and also buried in the sands of Graaff-Reinet.

Petrus Jacobus Fourie (40)[4]
Executed by firing squad at Graaff-Reinet on 19 August 1901.

Petrus Fourie was a 40-year-old farmer from Uitkomst in the Jansenville district. He appeared before the Military Court in Graaff-Reinet on 30 July 1901 and was described as a well-to-do and influential person. He was charged with high treason and the death of a coloured spy called

Petrus Fourie of Uitkomst, Jansenville.
Source: Hoe Zij Sterven

Christiaan. Furthermore it was alleged that he had caused the death of two British soldiers at Bloukrans and had burned down the Berrington house near Uitkomst. Fourie pleaded guilty to the charge of high treason but not guilty to the other charges. Witnesses gave evidence that he had joined the Scheepers commando and had been present at various skirmishes. However, no one could testify that he was responsible for the death of the spy. The black witnesses then stated that he was with the Boers at Uitkomst when the spy Christiaan was shot. The witnesses further confirmed that the said Christiaan was in British uniform and carried a weapon. No one could confirm that Fourie had shot the British soldiers or had been present at the Berrington house the day Christiaan was killed. The only fact established was that he had been captured with other Boers at Onbedacht by Scobell. Fourie was found guilty on all charges and condemned to death by firing squad.

Following his conviction, a former teacher at Jansenville, MF Fowler, wrote from his home in Warrington, England, that he had known Fourie to be a simple, soft-mannered man. He went on to state: 'Such stern acts of so-called justice will collate an antipathy to England which will be never dying, though possibly it may be crushed slowly out with the extermination of the Boer race. The blood of those simple farmers will cry to the Almighty for vengeance.'[5]

Fourie was executed together with Van Rensburg and Pfeiffer.

Jan van Rensburg (22)
Executed by firing squad at Graaff-Reinet on 19 August 1901.

This 22-year-old from Aberdeen was charged with the same crimes as Fourie at the Military Court in Graaff-Reinet. He too pleaded guilty only to the charge of high treason. The key witness for the prosecution was one Jan Momberg. Momberg had previously been sentenced to death but turned Crown witness in exchange for his life. His sentence was commuted to life imprisonment. Momberg, who also gave evidence in the Scheepers trial, insisted that he was forced to join the commandos against his will.[6] It was testified that Van Rensburg was present at a skirmish at Ouderplaats in May, when a British trooper was killed. Van Rensburg had a bandolier and carried a rifle. Furthermore, Van Rensburg was present at Murraysburg when the magistrates court and a house were burned down. He also stole a pair of police boots. He too was captured at Onbedacht by Scobell.

Van Rensburg received the death sentence for murder, arson and theft. He was executed with Fourie and Pfeiffer on the outskirts of Graaff-Reinet.

Lodewyk Francois Stephanus Pfeiffer
Executed by firing squad at Graaff-Reinet on 19 August 1901.

Pfeiffer, from the farm Leeufontein in the district of Victoria West, also appeared before the Military Court at Graaff-Reinet on 30 July, charged with high treason because he had been armed. Other charges included attempted murder because he had fired at British soldiers, as well as arson because he was alleged to have been present at the burning down of a farmhouse belonging to a Mr Heroldt in the Middelburg district. He was also one of those captured at Onbedacht.

Pfeiffer was found guilty on all charges and sentenced to death by firing squad. He was executed with Fourie and Van Rensburg on the Semelpoort heights outside Graaff-Reinet on 19 August 1901.

Jan van Rensburg of Aberdeen.
Source: Hoe Zij Sterven

Lodewyk Pfeiffer of
Loeriesfontein, Victoria-West.
Source: Hoe Zij Sterven

On 17 August, 13 rebels, including Fourie, Van Rensburg and Pfeiffer, were gathered on the church square at Graaff-Reinet for proclamation of sentence by Major H Schute. The sentences were ratified by Kitchener and they were to be executed together. The other sentences included death with clemency granted, banishment and jail terms. Once again the proceedings had to be attended by the populace as well as the 'undesirables'.

The sentences on Fourie, Van Rensburg and Pfeiffer were carried out simultaneously. The men were transported in an ambulance wagon early in the morning to Semelspoort, accompanied by the band of the Coldstream Guards. This place of execution is situated on the northern side of the heights on the road to Middelburg. Forty inhabitants of Graaff-Reinet received permits to witness the executions. Members of the Town Guards of Graaff-Reinet and Port Elizabeth were appointed guards. A company of 22 soldiers took up position opposite the condemned Boers. Each man was strapped to a chair in front of the open graves. They were rolled into blankets and slaked lime was poured over the bodies. At a distance, the Coldstream Guards band struck up a triumphful march.[7]

The executions of Fourie, Van Rensburg and Pfeiffer were the first for Graaff-Reinet. Scarcely a week later, the town was once again shaken by the executions of two youngsters, Daniël Olwagen and Ignatius Nel. Before the war ended, Graaff-Reinet would hear many more rifle volleys, with the executions of Hermanus Roux, Jacobus Geldenhuys and Gideon Scheepers.

In 1908, the remains of the seven burgers executed on the outskirts of Graaff-Reinet were exhumed. However, those of Commandant Scheepers were never found. On 1 December, they were laid to rest in a communal grave in the Graaff-Reinet cemetery.

Many people are unaware of this nameless grave in the old cemetery, with its simple headstone. On the day after the reburial, a commemorative monument bearing the names of the seven burgers was unveiled on the corner of Donkin and Somerset streets, on private property because both the town council and the Dutch Reformed Church refused to make a plot available for the erection of the monument. This peculiar decision by the Church and Town Council was intended to restore the peace in a town torn in two by the war. The unveiling of the monument was attended by 2 600 people, including Boer generals and commandants.[8]

CHAPTER 8

The Sins of
Two Lost Boys

Daniël F Olwagen (18)
Ignatius W Nel (17)
Executed by firing squad at Graaff-Reinet on 26 August 1901.

During the clash at Onbedacht, three young Boers were captured and sentenced to death by the Military Court sitting in Graaff-Reinet on 2 August 1901. The three lads faced similar charges of attempted murder. According to witnesses they belonged to a group of Boers who fired at the British soldiers. Olwagen and Nel were to die together on 26 August, while Hendrik Van Vuuren would be sent to Colesberg for execution.[1]

Two days before the executions in Graaff-Reinet were to take place the British commandant summonsed the Reverend Charles Daniel Murray of Petrusberg, the son of Reverend Charles Murray of Graaff-Reinet. The commandant told him that two more Boers were to be executed in Graaff-Reinet and that he was free to visit them in their cells.[2]

Reverend Murray first went to Daniël Olwagen and found him to be totally unprepared for what lay ahead. He described him as a fit young boy and well built. He told Olwagen about the prodigal son who confessed his sins and then returned to his father. The message he left with the distraught youngster was: 'Olwagen, man, let your nightly prayers be to ask the Lord to let you see your sins.'

The following day, Murray found a big difference in the boy, who believed that the Lord had revealed his sins to him.

After a long prayer session, Olwagen found forgiveness and peace

*Daniël Olwagen of
Graaff-Reinet.*
Source: Hoe Zij Sterven

*Ignatius Nel of Bulkraal,
Graaff-Reinet.*
Source: Hoe Zij Sterven

with himself. It was his desire to be welcomed by the Heavenly Father as the prodigal son had been welcomed by his father. When Murray departed, Olwagen said: 'Sir, the night will be long for me. I am in a hurry!'

Just before his execution, Murray visited him again. The boy was full of belief that the Lord would not leave him during his last moments. His face seemed to glow with serenity as he thought of the glorious life after death. They then fetched him to be executed.

After his visit to Olwagen, Murray entered the cell of Ignatius Nel. This physically strong youngster was six-foot tall and came from the farm Bulkraal in the Graaff-Reinet district. He had turned 17 a few days before. Nel was a retarded horse guard in the Scheepers commando and his execution carried undertones of the Claassen execution in Somerset East a month before. As he prayed for forgiveness for his sins, he was entirely unaware that he was about to die. Murray then noticed that his face was that of a young child. Nel could not understand why they had taken him away from his friends. Murray continues the story of their meeting:

'Good evening, Nel.'

'Sir, why have they locked me up all alone in here?'

'Friend, do you not know why you have been locked up in here?'

'No, Sir, I do not know what I have done!'

'Where were you this afternoon?'

'On the church square, Sir.'

'What did they do to you there?'

'Sir, they surrounded me with troops and took my hat off and read something in English. I do not understand English and I do not know what they read.'

'Did they not interpret it?'

'No, they just took me away and locked me up all alone in here!'

'Unbelievable, can you imagine that! This boy did not know that he had been sentenced to death! He was aghast and shattered when I had to tell him that he had to die on Monday!'

'What, Sir? To be shot? What did I do? I have never held a gun in my hand. I was a horse guard for a month with the commando. I never had a gun in my hand! Sir, I can swear before God and all my friends know that.'

'I could say nothing more to him except carry his plea to the Commandant who must give him a chance to prove his innocence. I then immediately hurried along to see the Commandant. The Commandant received me in a friendly manner and listened to what I had to say. He, however, cut our conversation short by declaring his regrets and informing me that subject was now closed. He furthermore informed me that once Kitchener, on advice from his law advisor, had ratified the sentence there was no right of appeal! He assured me that young Nel was guilty as charged. No matter how I pleaded for a stay of execution, it was to no avail.

'I returned to the cell of Nel and when the door opened he jumped up in expectation. Suddenly he turned around and sat down. His body started shaking and he could not utter a word. With great difficulty I convinced him that his sentence was irreversible and that he should channel his thoughts toward God.

'His knowledge of religion was slim. He had heard about God and Jesus, but knew nothing about the paternity of God and reconciliation through Christ. He was also unaware of the way to everlasting life, and within 36 hours he was to be there! Late at night we sat together in silence with my hand on his shoulder. This quiet presence of a fellow human eventually calmed him.'

Murray continued that he told young Nel the story of the prodigal son and that there was forgiveness for sins. In this manner he brought the gospel to the ailing boy. He asked the youngster to pray aloud after him: 'O my Father, I have committed many sins. Father, please forgive me.' After his confession and forgiveness he was no longer a pitiful, condemned person but a man full of faith and happiness.

When the bolts on the door were drawn the next morning he was not frightened, he smiled! He thanked the guards for putting the handcuffs on him. Danie Olwagen and Naas Nel climbed onto the ambulance wagon and greeted each other with glistening eyes. The wagon was accompanied by armed guards and was led onto the Murraysburg road. They proceeded through Van Ryneveld's Pass past the thorn trees to a place called De Krans. Murray spent a short time with them in prayer and they parted with firm handshakes.

'Now, farewell, I bid you,' said Murray.

'No, Sir, not farewell, but until we meet again,' replied Olwagen. On the ridge of the open graves they were bound to chairs. A detail of 20 Coldstream Guards took up position in front of the two boys. Moments after the command to fire, the medical officer pronounced them dead.

Murray concluded his account of the tragedy by saying: 'The two lost sons have arrived at their home.'

Both Olwagen and Nel were later reburied in the old Graaff-Reinet cemetery and their names appear on the Burger Monument in Donkin Street.

The particular emphasis that Reverend Murray placed on the confession of their 'terrible sins' underlines the outlook of certain Dutch Reformed Church ministers who believed that participation in the rebellion was against the scriptures. In a similar incident, the Reverend JC Kruger asked the condemned rebel Willie Kruger if it was not sinful to take up arms. The Boers interpreted this as being pro-British, and it may have been the reason why Gideon Scheepers refused to pray with the Reverend Charles Murray before his execution. Scheepers confirmed this in his diary, stating that he could not come to terms with the Reverend Murray because of his sympathy for the enemy![3]

The Church in the Cape could not formulate an official stand on the issue of rebels. Most of its ministers appeared to favour neutrality.[4] In time, some became pro-Boer while others would support the British war effort.[5]

The rebels executed in Graaff-Reinet are remembered on the Burger Monument in Donkin Street, Graaff-Reinet. They were executed along the main roads outside the town. Source/Photograph: Graham Jooste

A serious split occured in 1900 when the church council of the DRC in Graaff-Reinet ruled that services would no longer be held in English. The Reverend Charles Murray stated that in his 40 years of service he had never taken a chalice from God's hand as bitter as this one.[6]

On 17 August 1901, when the guerilla war was at its fiercest, Charles Murray and the British-minded Reverend JF Botha of Richmond obtained the signatures of 240 loyalists requesting President Steyn to withdraw all Free State forces from the Cape Colony.[7] Commandant Lötter advised Murray not to send him any more letters as he would view the carriers of these messages as spies. He urged Murray to remain neutral and not to stain his hands with the blood of innocent people.[8]

In September, Murray and Botha received permission from Kitchener to travel to the Free State to conduct meetings with President Steyn and General de Wet on this issue. Their mission was a complete failure and Steyn urged them to rather take their petition to Kitchener.[9] By the time they returned to the midlands, Lötter was behind bars as a result of the capture of his commando by Colonel Scobell.

After the war Murray received a gift from the loyalists of Graaff-Reinet for: 'Unswerving loyalty and for the valuable services rendered during the war.' Murray thanked them, and wrote: 'I never regretted having been loyal.'[10]

How deeply this wound cut into the Dutch Reformed Church is covered in a later chapter. The later execution of a minister's son, Willie Louw, prompted the comment that he was from 'the brood of Reverend Andrew Murray,' a minister who clashed with Milner over his strong pro-Boer sentiments.

CHAPTER 9

A Turn for Colesberg

Why three rebels sentenced to death in Graaff-Reinet were sent to Colesberg for execution remains a mystery. The evidence at the trials in Graaff-Reinet offers no reason for this strange decision of the Military Court. Why did two foreigners fighting for the Boers have to meet their destiny in Colesberg? The possibility exists that it was a result of Commandant Lötter and Field-Cornet Willie Louw, as well as many other rebels, originating from this area.

The fact that a German detachment played a decisive role in the defence of Colesberg earlier in the war could also have had a bearing on the decision. Perhaps the executions of the foreigners Veenstra and Toy would serve as a warning to all other foreigners who had ideas about supporting the Boer cause.

Whatever the reason, it was now without doubt the turn of Colesberg to receive its warning.

Hendrik Petrus van Vuuren (27)
Executed by firing squad at Colesberg on 4 September 1901.

Hendrik van Vuuren was captured with Ignatius Nel and Daniël Olwagen at Onbedacht. They appeared in the Military Court together and were charged with attempted murder. All three received the death sentence, but Van Vuuren was taken to Colesberg together with Veenstra and Toy to be executed. Though his comrades had been allowed to receive solace from a minister before their executions, this was not to be the case for Van Vuuren.

Hendrik van Vuuren was from the farm Hottentots River in the Willowmore district and joined the Scheepers commando in Aberdeen. Nothing more is known about this young man except that he did not understand a word of English and that his background was unknown. While in gaol he called out in the early hours of the morning to one Wilson to speak to him about his soul. Wilson said later that Van Vuuren was prepared to meet

Hendrik Petrus van Vuuren of Willowmore. Photograph/Source: Jozua van Vuuren, Pretoria

his God.[1] Hendrik van Vuuren perished at six minutes past seven on the morning of 4 September 1901, together with Toy and Veenstra, before a firing squad.

The medical certificate stated:

'I hereby certify that the death of Hendrik van Vuuren was caused by cardiac failure as a result of a gun-shot wound.'

MA Curry
Chief Surgeon
MO i/c Troops
COLESBERG

Van Vuuren's name appears on the Burger Monument in Colesberg. His grave is unknown. His grandson, Jozua van Vuuren of Pretoria, found a photograph of 'unknown rebels' in the Archives in Cape Town and sent it to us. His grandfather Hendrik van Vuuren appears in it.

Frederick Toy (Toe)
Executed by firing squad at Colesberg on 4 September 1901.

Toy was an artist from Gothenburg in Sweden and was resident in Johannesburg before the war. At its outbreak, he moved to the Cape Colony. During April 1901 he joined a Boer commando in the region of

Beaufort West. After only three months of service in the commando, he was captured together with a fellow foreigner, Hendrik Veenstra, and their leader, Lieutenant Izak Liebenberg, at Onbedacht in the Camdeboo near Graaff-Reinet. All three were later executed.[2]

During his court hearing, it was testified to that for the three months prior to his joining the commando he was resident in Willowmore. This was clearly a ploy by the prosecution to qualify him for rebel status. While the voters' roll was used in many instances to prove British citizenship, no mention of this procedure is to be found in the case of Frederick Toy. An example of this method will be found in the case of Commandant Lötter, who had to prove he was not a British citizen. In the case of Toy, he was listed in the Government Blue Book of convicted rebels as being from Gothenburg in Sweden, so certainly either a Transvaal burger or a Swedish national was executed by the British as a Cape rebel. A further charge was the attempted murder of Lieutenant Wynn of the 9th Lancers at Onbedacht.

Frederick Toy and Hendrik Veenstra were found guilty on 5 August on all charges by the Military Court in Graaff-Reinet and sentenced to death. Toy, Veenstra and Van Vuuren were transferred to Colesberg on 3 September and notified on the church square that they were to die the following day by firing squad.

Frederick Toy's name appears on the Burger Monument in Colesberg. His grave is unknown.

Hendrik Johan Veenstra (22)
Executed by firing squad at Colesberg on 4 September 1901.

Like Toy, Veenstra was a foreigner. This refined young Hollander was born in Amsterdam.

While in Holland, he attended the best schools and received numerous certificates, especially in the commercial sector. Upon his return to Holland he was to be employed by a French-Dutch company, which sent him out to South Africa for a holiday in 1899, just before the outbreak of hostilities. Unfortunately for Veenstra, the war delayed his return to Holland.[3]

During April 1901, he joined the commando of Commandant Scheepers. In documents placed before the Military Court his address

Frederick Toy of Gutenburg,
Sweden.
Source: Hoe Zij Sterven

Hendrik Veenstra of Amsterdam,
The Netherlands.
Source: Hoe Zij Sterven

was given as Rietfontein, Murraysburg. Three years later, he was captured with Lieutenant Liebenberg at Onbedacht in the Camdeboo. On 5 August he appeared in the Military Court in Graaff-Reinet, charged with being under arms and thus liable for high treason. He was further charged with the burning of three houses in the vicinity of Murraysburg, including the magistrates office, and with horse theft. He was found guilty on all charges and sentenced to death. He was executed as a rebel although it would have been impossible for him to attain British citizenship in the Cape Colony in such a short period of time.

Veenstra, Toy and Van Vuuren were transported to Colesberg and on 3 September they heard the proclamation of sentence on the church square. The internment of Reverend Scholtz did not help matters for the condemned men. An elder of the church, Meiring, asked for permission to visit the prisoners, but this was at first refused. The commandant had granted permission to an English priest to visit the condemned. Later Elder Meiring was granted permission for a visit.

The condition, however, was that he had to receive permission from the English priest. He, however, stated that he would only give his permission if the men asked for the elder. Nothing more was heard from the priest and the condemned men went to their graves without religious support. The evening before the execution, Veenstra wrote heartrending letters to his mother and family and to a Miss Ten Boom.

Colesberg, 3 September 1901
Approximately 8 o'clock in the evening

F van der Ahee, Esquire

Dear Uncle and cousins,
It is with a grieving heart that I am writing you a few lines to say farewell. It is not for myself that I feel sorrowful, thanks be to God. The loving Lord has given me the strength and mercy to be at peace with my allotted burden. Although it may sound terrible to those blood relatives that are left behind, I am longing for the hour that will finalise my sentence.

Do not grieve, loved ones, because it will certainly be better up there than here on earth. I have always prayed that His will be done and not mine. He protected me from the enemy's bullets during the fighting. He has granted me a short while in captivity to ponder over my sins and to expose them fully to Jesus ...

Therefore be not downhearted, because I hope, believe, trust and pray that Jesus is preparing a place for me in His Father's house. O, I hope and pray that I will see you all, yes all, there when your time has arrived ...

Now I face a difficult task, and that is to write to my mother. I would like you to put my mother's letter in an envelope with your letter. This would enable my mother to first read your letter so as to prepare her for the contents of my letter.

The prison warder will send to you about one pound four shillings, two gold rings and a raincoat. Uncle Goedhals would like the raincoat. The ring with the black stone I bequeath to you as a souvenir. The other ring must be sent back to my mother. She gave it to me. In Graaff-Reinet they took a photograph of me. It is my wish that you purchase five copies for 2/6 each and also send those home.

And now Uncle, you know what my mother's circumstances will be. Will you support her, you and Uncle Willem together? I thank you, Uncle, as well as your household, and also Uncle Willem and Aunt Mina and their household for surrounding me with their love and affection. Give my final farewells at Towerefontein, at Zadelsnaier and Middelfontein, to Aunt Gerdien and Uncle Manny and all the friends and acquaintances. And Judith, Heintje, Maria and Fransie to you as well.

From your Nephew,
Hendrik Jan Veenstra
I am sending my small Bible. Send it also to mother.

Colesberg Prison
3 September 1901

It is very difficult for me to write to you, but it is my duty to do so. May the Lord give you divine strength to be able to bear this just as He has given me the grace and strength to be resigned to my lot and to say that His will be done. The Lord is pleased to pluck me from this earth and to show me a place in His Father's house.

Being in prison for the last six weeks has been a struggle, but it has been my salvation because I have found the way to the Lord ... Therefore do not mourn because I am going on ahead and pray that one day you will all follow. I will not stop praying for you. O! let Garda and Sophia not stray from the right path. Let them love the Lord Jesus with all their heart because I have experienced what comfort and what strong courage it is to know that our Heavenly Father directs all our grief and pain ...

And now I thank you and Auntie as well as Miss B for all your prayers offered up for me. During these last days it has been of great comfort to me that so many sincere prayers have been said for me.

The Burger Monument in Colesberg with the names of those who fell in battle and five burgers who were executed. Photograph: Graham Jooste

Tomorrow morning at seven o'clock I will be entering eternity and even there I find comfort from the psalm:

'Although I tread in the valley of death,
And leave our earthly friends behind,
But He my friend and O! so kind,
Will be with us in our last breath!'

I wrote to Uncle Frans and asked him to return my ring to you as well as five photographs of myself. One is for you, one for Aunt Anna and one for Floris Vedenlof. The remaining two you will know what to do with ...

And now my beloved Mother and Aunt and Miss Ten Boom, I ask your forgiveness for all the grief I have caused you and for all your tears shed for me. Oh! I hope that all those I have sinned against will forgive me.

An English minister visited me and spoke to me in connection with John 14 and 15 and we prayed together. He promised to visit me again. A last farewell to my dear Mother and family, dear Aunt and dear Miss Ten Boom, family and friends and especially Floris.

I will pray for you all as you have prayed for me.
I see the portals open wide ...
By your Son, Brother, Nephew and friend,
Hendrik Jan Veenstra.
My little Bible will also be sent to you. Farewell until our blessed gathering in God the Father's house, my dear, dear Mother and Sisters.

The following morning the three prisoners were placed in an ambulance wagon and taken to the place of execution outside Colesberg. Open graves awaited them as they were bound to chairs upon the grave mounds. Twenty dollars lined up and fired the shots of death. Two died instantly while a third stayed alive for a while. As his head toppled over backwards, death claimed him. They were buried with the chairs. Upon orders the chairs were later removed and burnt.

Detailed below is a copy of a permit issued for the executions. It was written in longhand.

Colesberg
3/9/01
Mr L Kemper.

Sir,
If you wish to be present at the execution of the three prisoners condemned to death, please inform the Staff Officer in writing before 8 pm this day.

HD Lawrence. Capt.
Acting Commandant

This special permit stated as follows:

SPECIAL PERMIT

The bearer Mr L Kemper has leave to pass the examining guard on the Hanover road for the purpose of attending the execution of the condemned prisoners.
Frederick Toe
Hendrik J Veenstra
Hendrik van Vuuren
Who are sentenced to be shot.
The execution will take place on Wednesday the 4th instant at 7 am. All persons desiring to be present must have passed the examining guard by 6.45 am.

No persons will be allowed to pass the barrier after that hour. Absolute silence must be preserved.

Colesberg
3 Sept 1901
HD Lawrence
Capt
Acting Commandant.

The death certificates of both Veenstra and Toe were issued as follows:

CERTIFICATE

I hereby certify that sentence of death was carried out on the prisoner Frederick Toe at 6 min past 7 o'clock on this Wednesday 4th Sept 1901.

JF Hewell Smith. Lt. Col.
Area Cmdt. No 11 Area
Colesberg

Surgeon MA Curry issued the death certificate for Frederick Toe.

The *Graaff-Reinet Advertiser* reported as follows:

LATEST TELEGRAMS
Three Rebels shot at Colesberg
Colesberg 4th
This morning at 7 o'clock three Rebels were shot outside this town. Their names were: Frederick Toy, Jan Veemstra (sic), Hendrik van Vuuren. They were captured at the Camdeboo and tried at Graaff-Reinet.

Authors Note: Ref. Invitation and special permit, Colesberg Museum. Ref. Death certificates and press report, Cape Archives, Attorney-General's File AG 3560 and prisoner numbers 30, 31 and 34 Government Blue Book.

Their names appear on the Burger Monument in Colesberg, but the whereabouts of their graves are unknown.

CHAPTER 10

The Destruction of the Lötter Commando[1]

4 September 1901 was the day a new driving force was to be infused into the guerilla war in the Cape Colony. This was the day General Smuts entered the Colony to reorganise the various commandos. His dream had always been to unite the Cape Afrikaners in a mass uprising against the British. If he could achieve this objective, the Boers would have a third region supporting the cause. They would join forces with the Transvaal and Orange Free State. Furthermore, if this feat was successful then all Cape rebels would be classed as ordinary combatants and they could not be charged with treason.

4 September was also supposed to be the day when this dream was to be frustrated. On this day, the most important commando in the midlands was to meet with a devastating setback similar to that suffered by Scheepers in the Camdeboo. In the Tandjiesberg, Lötter was trapped and captured. This was the turning point for the Boer offensive in the Cape.

The now famed rebel-hunter Colonel Harry Scobell struck again. His columns, which had achieved success against Kritzinger and Scheepers, now delivered his greatest coup. He had faced many ordeals at the hands of other commando leaders but always maintained that Lötter was the most astute and dangerous of them all. He had been shadowing the Lötter commando for days across inhospitable terrain in the mountains between Cradock and Graaff-Reinet. Under his command the British columns adopted Boer methods. He abolished the use of cumbersome wagons and field-guns. Rations for his men were minimal and they were well armed. He also had detachments of Cape Colonial troopers with him who were familiar with the Boers and their tactics. A further advantage was that he was able to procure fresh mounts along the way. For days he followed the Boers on their spent and tired horses.

Colonel Harry Scobell.
Photograph: After Pretoria, *by Wilson*

Exhausted, hungry and weakened by a heart ailment, Lötter led his men in torrential rain to safety at Bouwershoek. This area was deep in the Tandjiesberg and close to a hamlet called Petersburg. In a large sheep enclosure on the farm Paardefontein the bedraggled Boers dismounted and rested. After many days of riding they had been unable to dislodge Scobell from their trail. The entrance to the kloof was protected by prickly-pear bushes and it would be impossible for a cavalry to come over the mountains in the rain. Lötter was so confident that he placed only a few guards at the entrance of the kloof and none on the side of the mountain. The guards soon found shelter from the rain. Luck was to be with them; they alone escaped the carnage that was to follow.

Lötter thought that he had escaped from the flying column and had ample time to set up camp. At midnight Scobell abandoned his packmules and led his tired and hungry troops over the mountain. In pouring rain and wind they descended slippery animal paths and steep inclines to reach the heights protecting the hamlet of Petersburg and Lötter. Many of the mounts had to be freed as the troops continued on foot. At sunrise they could see Lötter's camp and silently took up their positions.

The exact location of Lötter's camp was betrayed by one Lewies van Niekerk, enabling Scobell to attack early that morning. The entire commando was trapped inside the kraal and only a quarter of the Boers could return fire after the British fusillade.

In the attack, 14 Boers were killed and 126 captured, including 52 wounded. Only the 19 guards escaped.[2] Both Lötter and the reliable Wolfaardt received serious wounds. Scobell mentioned in his diary that the butchery and the ghastly wounds he saw would remain with him for the rest of his life. The Boers had fought 'as men will who know they have ropes round their necks'. After half an hour those who had survived were huddled together in a corner of the kraal. The dead and wounded were strewn everywhere. A correspondent of the *Graaff-Reinet Advertiser* reported that had the Boers delayed their surrender by white flag a minute later there would have been no survivors! Ten British soldiers were killed and eight received wounds.

A day after the ambush Lötter's commando, accompanied by a large guard detachment, were paraded through Graaff-Reinet. Scobell's troops received a heroes' welcome. The streets were festooned with bunting, crowds assembled and the Coldstream Guards cheered their columns. Praise and congratulations were showered upon Scobell from near and far, as well as from England. A telegram later received at headquarters read: 'The King has approved your promotion to Brevet Colonelcy.' According to Scobell, it was his proudest day of the guerilla campaign. He stated that he regarded Lötter as a 'most dangerous man' as well as being the best of General Kritzinger's commanders.

Scobell's columns escort Lötter's commando through the streets of Graaff-Reinet to prison after the whole commando had been captured. The wounded can be seen on the wagons.
Source: Graaff-Reinet Museum

Three weeks later the Military Court started its hearings. Lötter's commando consisted mainly of Cape rebels, who could expect the worst. The majority were banished to Bermuda while many received life sentences. Many were sentenced to death but later received clemency and were confined to prison with hard labour. Five ranking Boers were, however, to face firing squads at various towns in the midlands. They were:[3]

Commandant JC Lötter	Executed at Middelburg on 12/10/1901
Lieutenant PJ Wolfaardt	Executed at Middelburg on 15/10/1901
Lieutenant JG Schoeman	Executed at Tarkastad on 12/10/1901
Commandant DC Breed	Executed at Cradock on 17/10/1901
Field-Cornet WS Kruger	Executed at Cradock on 17/10/1901

Lötter (centre, seated on a chair) and members of his commando.
Wolfaardt is squatting front left.
Source: War Museum of the Boer Republics

Five teenagers also received death sentences, but these were altered to internment for the duration of the war on Kitchener's orders. However, the boys would each receive between 20 to 25 strokes with a cane. The exception would be the young Van Meynen who would receive only 12 strokes because of his extreme youth. They were:

Hermanus van Meynen (14)

Johannes du Plessis (16)
Stephanus Cornelius Schoeman (17)
Johannes Jurgen Lotter (17)
Christiaan Johannes Hendrik van Heerden (19)

These horrible death sentences, then the clemencies, followed by the corporal punishments, could only be a strong message to the youth of the midlands not to take part in the guerilla activities of the rebels. The sentences administered to the youths had nothing to do with justice, because the entire commando was guilty of high treason, and many of its members were liable for the death sentence.

Commandant Johannes Cornelius Lötter (26)
Executed by firing squad at Middelburg on 12 October 1901.

Lötter was born in 1875 on the farm Bouwersfontein in the district of Somerset East. Like thousands of his contemporaries he moved from the Cape Colony and took up citizenship in the Orange Free State. After a long sojourn in the Free State, he moved to Noupoort in the Cape, a short while before hostilities broke out, when he opened a business. Early in November 1899 when the Boer commandos entered Colesberg, he was seen at Rosmead near Middelburg, at the Railway hotel, belonging to Mrs Elworthy. It appears that he was bartending, and that night sang patriotic Transvaal freedom songs on the veranda. The next morning he and his horse disappeared.

Lötter joined the commando at Colesberg and served under Commandant Kritzinger in the Free State. With the second invasion by Boer forces of the Colony he was involved with Kritzinger during various operations. He progressed quickly and was promoted to commandant. Lötter and Scheepers busied themselves in the midlands by wrecking railway lines, thus hampering the movements of British troops and communications. They had become known for their ingenuity, audacity and daredevil escapes. When Kitchener instituted his scorched-earth and concentration-camp policies, General De Wet gave the commandos permission to retaliate. Among the targets for retribution would be loyalists, traitors, spies and armed blacks.[5] The two commandants went about this task adroitly and with zeal. Loyalists' houses were burned, traitors were whipped, trains looted and spies executed. The actions made them the two most sought-after guerilla leaders in the Colony.

On the charge sheets in the Military Court these acts were described as 'murder, marauding and disgraceful conduct of a cruel nature', and therefore the charges were of war crimes and violations of human rights. In the Transvaal and Free State similar deeds committed by the British, which included the razing of farmhouses, plundering, destruction of herds of livestock, detention of women and children in the concentration camps and execution of spies, were looked upon as normal warfare in a civilised war!

Commandant Lötter of Colesberg after he was captured.
Photograph: War Museum of the Boer Republics

Therefore the only valid crime of which Lötter could have been found guilty was that of being a Cape rebel and thus liable for high treason. The burning issue in his trial was whether he was a Free Stater or a British subject. As will be seen later this was a futile attempt by the Military Court to lend some credibility and justice to the case. No proof of citizenship was ever needed in the trials of Scheepers, Breed and Liebenberg, who were all Republican citizens. They were executed as Free State and Transvaal citizens found guilty of war crimes.

Lötter was brought before the Military Court in Graaff-Reinet on 27 September 1901. Apart from the main charge of being active in arms against Her Majesty's forces, he was accused of the murder of two black spies, the flogging of three loyalists with a *sjambok*, three charges of detonating railway lines, robbery and theft. However, the longest part of the proceedings concerned his citizenship.

The court maintained that he was registered as a voter in Colesberg and that he was resident in the Cape Colony when he had joined the Boer forces. In his defence Lötter stated that the name that appeared on the Colesberg voters' roll was not his. He referred to the difference in the Christian names and was adamant that he had never registered in that town. He went on to explain that his Free State citizen document was in a small case, which was lost or destroyed the day of surrender. Witnesses for the defence gave evidence that they had seen these papers. British intelligence stated that it could find no proof of his Free State citizenship in Bloemfontein. Lötter responded by asking how he could prove his citizenship when all his witnesses were still on commando and that he had been granted no time to call upon them.

The Military Court rebuffed these arguments and also overlooked the fact that Lötter had been resident in the Free State for many years before the war. Many Boers who had gone to the Free State from the Colony and stayed there never formally applied for citizenship. Lötter's plea that he was in fact a Free Stater failed and he was sentenced to death as a Cape rebel. His sentence was ratified by Kitchener on 7 October. He was transferred to Middelburg and heard the proclamation of sentence read on 11 October in the street adjoining the town square. It was a most impressive ceremony. The Middelburg Town Guard, the District Mounted Troops and the Royal Fusileers took up positions around the town square. A large crowd had gathered on the square as all places of business were compelled to close. Attendance by the inhabitants was obligatory.

A scene at Lötter's trial showing him in the dock.
Source: Graaff-Reinet Museum

Lötter (centre, with arms folded) listens to his sentence on the church square in Middelburg. Source: After Pretoria, *by Wilson*

At exactly 12 noon Lötter appeared on the square with an armed escort of guards. His hands were manacled and he appeared to be tired and ill as a result of his wounds. He listened to the proclamation of sentence in a calm manner, but fainted immediately after it was completed. After he revived he was hauled back to prison to await the following day when he would be executed. A certain Miss N, in all probability a close friend, received permission to visit him in his cell. She recalls this visit:

'Mr V and myself made our way through a mass of Khakies carrying rifles with fixed bayonets. We so wanted to be with him to console him. In the cell we did not find a person given in to despair because of illness and wounds but a young man lying on his bed in a calm and resigned manner. He asked me to sit down beside him and thanked us for coming. He told Ben he could have a smoke but that he did not feel like one. Immediately afterwards he changed his mind and said: "Yes brother, this will be our last smoke"! Before he lit up, he looked at me and asked, "Miss N, with your permission"? I just nodded my head because words failed me. When he noticed my sorrow he said: "Oh, no, Miss N, do not be sad for me, I am prepared to go. It is the will of God. My only regret is that I will not be able to see the fruits of my labour but instead I will find peace. Peace for my soul? Yes I have that, but the peace of my land and nation will be hidden from me".'

She then gave him two small prayer books and together they read from them. After they were finished he said: 'If God was not my helper then I would be lost! I receive such joy when I think of eternity and what awaits me, not in future years but only in a few hours from now.

Tomorrow when the sun rises so will my big sun come up. Sister, let me tell you that a person cannot remain an Afrikaner unless he becomes a child of God. Because they will try to lead you astray, threaten you with cruelty and try to bribe you. It is then that God the Father must help.'

'When the time for parting came he wanted to give me a keepsake, but as he had nothing he cut off a lock of his hair with his penknife. He gave it to me and said: "Everything is now ready. I only have to greet my dear lady friend." He then kissed me cordially and said: "God be with you until we meet again." I asked him if it was the will of God that his men were all in a deplorable condition? He answered sincerely: "Oh no, I have never had any regrets of the path I chose. It is justifiable before God and I was called to it."

'Did you not expect the death sentence when you collapsed at the market square? The thought had come to me.

' "Oh yes, but do not forget, my physical strength was drained. Furthermore they have starved me and with my heart problem the thought of death overwhelmed me. My mother appeared before my eyes ... Oh, I feel so sorry for her".

'A voice from behind the cell door announced: "Your time is up!" When we left his words still echoed in our ears: "God be with you ...".'

Reverend S Postma and Reverend JF Le Clus also obtained permission to visit Lötter and Le Clus was allowed to be with him at his execution. Outside Middelburg on the road to Richmond, Lötter was executed by firing squad tied to a chair.

From his death cell, Lötter wrote this letter to his family.

Middelburg. 11 October 1901

Dearest Mother, Father, Brothers and Sisters,
Herewith I would like to advise you all that I have recently received the death sentence. Be comforted Mother, Father, Brothers and Sisters. The Lord said that not a hair from our head shall fall without His will. I am fully prepared and satisfied to meet my Lord.

Receive my greetings, not forever, because we will meet again afterwards.

I remain your son,
JC Lötter

At Lötter's request, Reverend Le Clus also wrote a letter to his mother consoling her. He assured her that Lötter was completely resigned to his fate, that in his faith in his Saviour he remained calm to the end and that in this faith he received the grace to forgive his enemies.

In 1907 Lötter, Wolfaardt and Marais were reburied in the Middelburg cemetery where a monument in commemoration of them was erected. The remains of Lötter and Wolfaardt were placed in one coffin. All three names appear on the Burger Monument situated in the town square. At the place where Lötter and Wolfaardt died before a firing squad on the Richmond road, the well-known Chair Monument was built of stone.

Lieutenant Pieter Jacobus Wolfaardt (32)
Executed by firing squad at Middelburg on 15 October 1901.

This 32-year-old rebel was Johannes Lötter's friend and right-hand man. They were captured together at Paardefontein.[7]

Wolfaardt was a married man with small children who farmed at Fair View in the Middelburg district. He joined the commando on 6 February during the Boer's second excursion into the Colony. Wolfaardt's charge sheet describes him as a man of influence and of a truculent nature. His bravery and recklessness often had to be curtailed by his fellow burgers. During his trial 'his firm attitude displayed him as a person who regarded his Afrikaner heritage as paramount. He would not divulge any information even when he received fine promises'. The only defence that he offered was that he had been influenced by the large-scale arming of blacks by the British. Also, the shocking martial law regulations and the total suppression of the people, including the cruel treatment of women and children in the concentration camps, appalled him. He often referred to the fact that he would never have taken up arms had it not been for these happenings.[8] It was testified that he had shot two troopers at point-blank range and wounded another before blood from a wound received covered his face. Wolfaardt was tried with Willie Kruger at Graaff-Reinet on 27 September 1901 and sentenced to death for murder and attempted murder. On 11 October the proclamation of sentence was made together with that of Lötter at the church square in Middelburg. He heard his sentence with the calmness he had often displayed on the battlefields.

Lötter and Wolfaardt shackled together shortly before being executed at Middelburg.
Photograph: Mrs. LP Loest of Rouxville

His family was allowed to visit him in prison. His weeping wife entered the cell and he embraced her and calmed her down. He thanked the Lord that he had been spared long enough to enable him to see her again. When she sobbingly asked him if he was prepared to die, he answered: 'Yes, absolutely.'

Pieter Wolfaardt of Fair View, Middelburg.
Source: Hoe Zij Sterven

After a first refusal he was later allowed to see his eldest son, Pieter, who meant much to him. When it was time for them to leave his cell he offered up a powerful prayer to the Lord and placed his family in His care. He was executed three days after Lötter at the same place alongside the Richmond road. Both Reverend Le Clus and Elder Postma accompanied him on his last journey. He assured them that all was well with him. After he was blindfolded and tied to the chair he uttered the words: 'Safe in the arms of Jesus' just before the volley from the firing squad struck him down. He died fearless in death, as in life.

His name appears on the Burger Monument on the town square together with those of Lötter and Marais. On the Chair Monument his name appears with that of his leader and friend, Hans Lötter.

Commandant Dirk C Breed[9]

Executed by firing squad at Cradock on 17 October 1901.

About the citizenship of Dirk Breed there is no doubt at all. He was a Free Stater from Bethulie. On the group photograph of prisoners taken at Graaff-Reinet his address is given as Bethulie, Orange River Colony. Shearing described him as 'The wild Free Stater'. Therefore he could not be charged as a rebel and his name does not appear in the Cape Government Blue Book listing rebels. He thus had to be charged and tried for war crimes. That he could have been found guilty of any crime greater than those committed by any line soldier, British or Boer, remains uncertain. As a Free State citizen, he faced the only charge the British could trump against him, and that was for murder.

Breed, a widower, joined the Kritzinger commando during the second invasion of the Cape Colony by Boer forces. When Kritzinger was forced to retire across the Orange River he left Breed behind in the Stormsberg.

The 'Chair Monument' erected in memory of Lötter and Wolfaardt outisde Middelburg at the place where they were executed by firing squad. The words at the top of the monument read: 'What does this stone mean to you?' Joshua 4:6.
Photograph: Graham Jooste

DC Breed of Bethulie
Orange Free State

He held the rank of lieutenant, and his main duty was to find recruits and mobilise the district. He blew up a train close to Stormsberg station and was involved in numerous skirmishes with British columns, penetrating as far as Lady Grey before joining Lötter in the Cape Midlands. During this period he must have attained the rank of commandant because at his trial he was referred to as such. He was trapped and captured with Lötter at Paardefontein.

On 26 September 1901 he and Wilhelm Stephanus Kruger were brought before the Military Court at Graaff-Reinet on charges of attempted murder and murder. They both received death sentences and were executed together at Cradock on 17 October. Breed, a fiery Republican, was concerned about his beloved Free State. He strongly believed that the British would be beaten. When asked by Reverend JC Kruger if he was afraid of death, he answered: 'I was miraculously spared by the Lord during the war. It is now His will that I should die for my country and people. I am ready to meet Him.'

At the grave his firm handshake and bright countenance were long remembered by Reverend Kruger. He died like a man for his country as did so many others. Before his execution, Breed wrote to his mother from his prison cells.

Graaff-Reinet. 9 Oct. 1901
Mrs WC Breed

Dear and loving Mother, Brothers and Sisters,
It is with a tender heart that I advise you that all is well with me. My hope is that it is the same with you. Further I must tell you that I am in captivity.

Dearest Mother, Brothers and Sisters, you must always keep the Lord before your eyes. Seek Him with haste and do not wait until it is too late. Mother, be comforted. Everything will be fine.

Being in internment has converted me from my sins. I feel happy because I have met my God. It is wonderful to be with Him because then one's burden is not all that heavy. The heaviest sentence is nothing. The Lord said that whoever built on him did not build on sand ... I must end my letter now, but not with my longing heart.

With best greetings
from your child.
DC Breed

A group photo of rebels in the prison at Graaff-Reinet. Dirk Breed is No. 67.
Source: Graaff-Reinet Museum

Field-Cornet Wilhelm Stephanus Kruger (34)[10]
Executed by firing squad at Cradock on 17 October 1901.

Willie Kruger was a married man with four small children. A farm manager for Danie Michau at Juriesdam in the Cradock district, he joined the Lötter commando, which was overrun by Scobell at Paardefontein on 5 September 1901. During this bloody encounter he

Willie Kruger of Juriesdam, Cradock.
Source: Hoe Zij Sterven

received five wounds and saw his brother die next to him. He was captured, and tried for high treason, murder and attempted murder of British soldiers by the Military Court together with Dirk Breed at Graaff-Reinet on 26 September and sentenced to death. He was confined to prison in Graaff-Reinet before being taken to Cradock for his execution with Breed on 17 October.

Kruger was an extremely religious man who looked upon it as his duty to lead souls to the Lord. In his younger days he held prayer meetings and would often pray alone in the veld. Reverend Kruger, who visited him in gaol, stated that he had a strong religious influence over the commando members, many of whom stated that it was Kruger who had led them to the Lord, including his fellow prisoner, Dirk Breed. Upon being asked by Reverend Kruger if he had committed sin by becoming a Rebel (see Chapter 8), Kruger answered:

Breed and Kruger are sentenced to death on the market square in Cradock.
Source: After Pretoria, *by Wilson*

'No, the only driving force behind me to rise up was the suffering of the women and children. I am convinced that God led towards that.' Kruger asked him later to open his heart because soon he would be standing before his God and, 'Then it will be the truth'.

After a prayer it was Kruger's wish that a message of thanks be conveyed to the Reverend CD Murray of Petrusville for his preaching, which had always been a joy to him.

Kruger was visited by his wife and their four small children, together with his mother, three sisters and a cousin, but they were prevented from giving him the sweets they had brought. He placed his mother in the care of his wife and asked his children to obey their mother, telling them that he would be waiting for them in heaven. During his final night he wrote to his wife:

Cradock (Prison)
The 16th October 1901

A word of consolation to my loved one.
As you know it was God's calling to the work that I had to do. I tried to be faithful as a daily labourer and the hand of God was upon me. Oh! my beloved, do not mourn my passing. My cup is full and shall I not drink from that which my Father has given me? Oh! my beloved, my pilgrimage into eternity is almost completed ... I drink from the cup. It is bitter. It is hard for flesh and blood but Jesus drank it to the dregs for me. Oh! my beloved, I think back to the pleasant days we spent together over the last fourteen years. Oh! how sweet was our life together. But Oh, how glorious it will be with Jesus! There we will meet friends who have gone before. Let us cling to eternal things. God stands by His word. He leaves no prayer unanswered. God helps us all to hold onto his promises.

> The grief which comes is for the heart,
> Steadfast the word upon His part.
> No matter how rugged the way we see,
> The end is surely blessed to be.

WS Kruger

At 6 am the following day Kruger and Breed were led out to the waiting ambulance wagon. It made its way along the Orange River banks to a place called Geregsplaas (place of execution), outside Cradock. Guards with rifles and fixed bayonets rode before and behind the wagon. The procession came to a halt before two freshly dug graves. The Reverend Kruger accompanied the men towards their final resting places. They both assured him that they would open their eyes before the glory of God. They thanked Kruger and shook hands with him. The firm handshake and staring eyes of Breed would never be forgotten by this gentleman. They were bound to the chairs and blindfolded. The firing squad commander asked them if they had said their prayers and gave the command to open fire.

Breed was hit in the chest, toppled over forward and appeared to live for a few more seconds. Kruger received shots through the head, jerked backwards and died instantly. They were rolled into blankets and buried. Their graves are somewhere along the banks of the Orange River on the outskirts of Cradock. Both are remembered on the monument in the Dutch Reformed Church garden of Cradock.

Lieutenant Jacobus Gustavus Schoeman (31)[11]
Executed by firing squad at Tarkastad on 12 October 1901.

During the engagement at Paardefontein in which the Lötter commando was attacked by Scobell's forces, Schoeman was one of the Boers captured in a donga. Lieutenant D Bowers of the Cape Mounted Rifles testified that fire from the donga resulted in many British deaths. JP du Plessis, a scab-inspector from Tarkastad turned British spy, stated that

Jacobus Schoeman of Groot Zeekoegat, Tarkastad.
Source: From a group photo in Graaff-Reinet Museum

he knew Schoeman and that he was with the rebels captured at Paardefontein. He could however not confirm that Schoeman was armed. WP Louw of Pearston gave evidence that Schoeman was with those who stole two horses from him.

Scobell's success can be attributed to the colonial troops in his command who knew the areas of conflict well. Furthermore, he relied heavily upon information obtained from spies who were seconded to his intelligence staff. Many of them knew the rebels well as they had lived among them.

Schoeman was found guilty of murder

and theft by the Military Court at Graaff-Reinet and sentenced to death on 17 September. The inadequacy of the witnesses was commented upon by the Advocate-General's Office, which reviewed the case after sentence had been passed: 'There is of course no direct proof of his (Schoeman) having shot any of the British killed.' After his trial Schoeman was transferred to his home town of Tarkastad. He was to remain in gaol for a month to await the outcome. On 11 October his death sentence was proclaimed in the town. The next morning, a weak and pale Schoeman was helped by two soldiers on his way to execution.

The saga of Jacobus Schoeman is recalled in the introductory passages of this book. His grave is unknown and no tombstone or monument bearing his name has been found. In the only known photograph of him, taken by IB Allan, he appears among a group of captured Boers in Graaff-Reinet. An unknown photographer did, however, photograph him being tied to a chair somewhere outside Tarkastad, probably the same person who captured the dramatic scene of the execution of Pieter van Heerden at Tarkastad exactly one month later.

A group photograph of rebels in the prison at Graaff-Reinet. Two of them were executed by firing squad: Jacobus Schoeman (No. 40) at Tarkastad and Pieter Wolfaardt (No. 46) at Middelburg. The 14-year-old youngster, Hermanus van Meyen (No. 27) was sentenced to death, but his sentenced was commuted to 12 cuts with a cane.

CHAPTER 11

Captured in Khaki

It was a ragged commando led by General Jan Smuts that reached the Tarkastad district after an epic ride through the Free State and over the Stormsberg. They were in tatters, wrapped in blankets which served as clothing along with grain bags and skins. Their need for clothing was thus far greater than for horses and ammunition. In the Elands River gorge near Tarkastad, their luck changed when they came upon a detachment of 17th Lancers, which formed part of Scobell's command.

The camp was surprised on the misty morning of 17 September, captured and overwhelmed, and the British forced to surrender. Here Smuts replenished his weary commando with food, horses, ammunition and khaki uniforms. Unaware of the proclamation by French stating that any burger caught in British uniform would be executed, a jubilant commando, refreshed and clothed, continued into the Cape Midlands.

Five burgers were to pay the ultimate price for being captured wearing this clothing: Piet de Ruyt, Henry Rittenberg, Cornelius Vermaas, Arie van Onselen and Jack Baxter.

Piet de Ruyt[1]
Summarily executed at Glen Lynden, Bedford district, during September 1901.

Born in Holland, De Ruyt was the first to be caught in khaki uniform, in a wayside inn at Glen Lynden in the Bedford district. A few of the Boers, possibly a scouting detail, spent the night at the small hotel. After so many dry months the hotel bar was a great temptation. Early the next morning the group left, later realising that De Ruyt was not with them, having been left behind, sleeping off a hangover. According to Deneys Reitz in his book *Commando*, De Ruyt was shot out of hand when captured because he was wearing a khaki uniform. De Ruyt was probably buried near the hamlet, but no grave could be found.

Cornelius Vermaas (20)
Henry Rittenberg (20)
Arie van Onselen (22)
Summarily executed near Glen Connor in the Uitenhage district on
3 October 1901.[2]

When Smuts crossed the Suurberg mountains to continue his raid into the Cape Colony his scouts were very active. These three young Transvalers were ordered to reconnoitre along the Sundays River and and around Glen Connor and to scout along the road leading to the coast. On 2 October they crossed the Osberg mountain at Brakkefontein and made their way cautiously towards the Kariega railway siding. Arie van Onselen knew this area well as he had been brought up here by his foster parents before departing for the Transvaal. They were apparently

The inn along the main route to Baviaanspoort in the vicinity of Bedford where De Ruyt died. Photograph: Graham Jooste

Cornelius Vermaas of Losberg, Transvaal.
Source: Huisgenoot, 12 January 1945

on their way to visit Van Onselen's foster parents when they rode straight into a British column, all three still wearing the uniforms they had taken from the 17th Lancers.

Vermaas was badly wounded. His friends rushed to his aid and also received wounds. They were surrounded and captured and immediately shot in cold blood. This story was later related by a colonial trooper who was a member of the British column.

The incident was confirmed in a despatch by General French to Lord Roberts wherein he stated that any Boer found wearing a khaki uniform would suffer immediate execution. He notified Roberts that they had executed three recently.[3]

The three burgers were buried in a communal grave on the slopes of the Osberg at the place where they were executed.[4] Two years after the war, the brother of Cornelius Vermaas exhumed his brother's remains

Arie van Onselen, previously of Kruisrivier in the Zuurberg Mountains.
Source: Huisgenoot, 12 January 1945

and had them buried in the Uitenhage cemetery. An ornamental tombstone was erected over the grave. He was unable to obtain permission to remove the remains of the other two men. A year later the foster parents of Arie van Onselen received such permission and they removed their adopted son as well as the remains of Henry Rittenberg. They were buried in a small cemetery near the Kariega railway siding. On Heroes' Day in 1944 a tombstone was erected over their graves with the stirring epitaph: 'They died so that our ideal of freedom can live.' The epitaph for

The broken memorial column on the grave of Cornelius Vermaas in the cemetery at Uitenhage. (The names of Rittenberg and Van Onselen appear on the other side.) Photograph: Dr J de Swardt

The grave of Arie van Onselen and Henry Rittenberg at Kariega Halt near Glenconnor. Source: Huisgenoot, 12 January 1945

Cornelius Vermaas in the Uitenhage cemetery is a lament for those left behind: 'Here rests our Cornelius. He died a hero's death on his birthday the 2nd of October 1901. With him fell his friends Henry Rittenberg and Arie van Onselen.'

John (Jack) Alexander Baxter (22)[5]
Summarily executed at Goewermentsvlei, Aberdeen district, on 13 October 1901.

John Alexander Baxter was born in Newcastle, Natal, and named after his grandfather the Reverend John Baxter, who came from England. After his execution, his father wrote:

'He was always an obedient son. I cannot recall that I ever had to punish him. He was a polite boy and excelled at school. He was a brave lad and very kindhearted. I remember the day he brought home two dead lambs; he was crying bitterly. I had trouble in comforting him. When he was sixteen he found employment with the Telegraph Department in Johannesburg. He later joined the customs at Elandsfontein before his transfer to the head office in Pretoria.

'When the war broke out he realised he would not be accepted in

John (Jack) Baxter of Ermelo, Transvaal.
Source: Hoe Zij Sterven

Pretoria as he had weak eyesight and was not strong. He left for Klerksdorp and joined the commando of General Liebenberg. On 12 November 1901 I was handed a letter from Captain Powell in Volksrust from my son. He informed me that he had been captured by the English and was wearing khaki. Because of this he had been sentenced to death. Furthermore he asked us not to grieve for him because he was sure of an eternally blessed life.'

Early one morning the young Baxter was returning to his commando after standing watch during the night on the farm Goewermentsvlei in the Aberdeen district. He never got back to his camp. On the way he stopped and enquired of a shepherd as to the whereabouts of his camp. The shepherd directed him towards the British columns, because he was dressed in khaki.

He rode off without concern and ambled into the British camp, perhaps because of his weak eyesight, or he could have confused the 17th Lancers' uniforms with those of his comrades.[6] Whatever the reason, he was surprised as they were, and arrested.

Various members of the Smuts commando had escaped from hazardous situations as Scobell's column mistook them for British troops. It must also be pointed out that Captain Watson of the 17th Lancers had recently been killed in a skirmish where the British troops mistook the Boers for their own soldiers. These incidents sealed young Baxter's fate.

Baxter was tried by a Military Court set up immediately in the veld, found guilty of wearing a khaki uniform and condemned to death. The fact that Baxter was English also counted heavily against him. However, Scobell was very impressed with the young man, and wrote in his diary:

'The prisoner was dressed in khaki. He was a nice, smart-looking young chap by name Baxter and I am sure an Englishman, though he declared that he was German. He was an extraordinary good plucked chap. Never even changed colour when I told him his sentence, just asked for paper and pencil and wrote letters all the time. I saw the job through and, as he sat on a box to be shot, I couldn't help shaking hands with him, telling him how sorry I was and how much I admired his bravery. He said: "I am all right. Don't bother about me. We are both soldiers and have to die sooner or later. I am not afraid to die." Thirty seconds later he was dead.'[7]

Before his execution Baxter asked for a pipe and a pinch of tobacco. He also enjoyed a glass of whisky with Scobell. After he was granted time to write a letter to his father he knelt down in prayer. The letter to his parents was short and precise:

EA Baxter Esq.
Amsterdam
Ermelo (Transvaal)

Dear Parents,
I was captured as a prisoner of war this morning and sentenced to death for wearing khaki clothes. Do not be filled with grief, my dear parents, because it is the will of the Lord and I will enter into death with the knowledge that I will be with Him from now and to eternity. I left my Will with HS Esquire in Klerksdorp.
God bless you all.

Greetings from your loved one.
JA Baxter

In one of his letters he thanked he thanked his commandant, Ben Bouwer, and his fellow commando members for their loyalty. He urged them not to find sadness in his death and told them that he would die without being blindfolded. When he was taken to his place of execution he first saluted the officers, then joined the ranks like a British soldier and marched with them to the chosen spot. At the graveside Baxter refused to sit on a box or to be blindfolded, saying that he would die like a man. Scobell granted his requests and told him to turn around. Four bullets struck him in the back of the head. As a sign of respect, they left him where he fell for two hours.

The soldiers later returned and wrapped his body in a blanket and buried him. At least he received the burial of a soldier and not that of a rebel. The following official notification of Baxter's execution appeared in the Transvaal:

A Boer prisoner named JA Baxter was captured by Colonel Scobell's column on about 14 October. He was brought before a court martial because he was wearing khaki clothes so as to mislead Her Majesty's troops. He was found guilty and executed immediately. It was his wish that the enclosed letter be handed over.

(Witness) AL Powell, Captain
Volksrust, 12/11/1901

After the war, General Smuts, who was famed for his reconciliatory attitude towards the British, never forgave Scobell for the cruel treatment meted out to Baxter. He stated on many occasions that the Boers did not wear khaki to deceive the English, but that they had no other clothes and would have otherwise had to fight naked. At the peace negotiations at Vereeniging, Smuts refused to shake Scobell's hand. Years later, when Smuts was Minister of Defence and Scobell was the commanding officer of the British troops in the Cape, Smuts maintained this attitude and refused to meet Scobell. On the other hand, Scobell put the blame squarely on the shoulders of Smuts and insisted that he should have alerted his commandos to the danger of being caught wearing khaki.[8]

In 1938 CJC Weitz of Aberdeen pointed out the grave of Jack Baxter on Goewermentsvlei next to the gravel road to Murraysburg. He was a 12-year-old boy at the time and had seen Baxter buried.

Baxter's grave in the cemetery
at Aberdeen.
Photograph: Graham Jooste

The remains of Jack Baxter were exhumed under the guidance of Reverend Gert Barnard, placed on a wagon drawn by mules and reburied in the Aberdeen cemetery. His well-looked-after grave is to be found there, next to him the graves of other fallen Boers. His spectacles, enlarging glass, comb and spoon, as well as a few buttons that were found in his grave, are in the care of the Aberdeen Primary School. His name appears on the Burger monument in Ermelo.[9]

CHAPTER 12

The Brood of
Andrew Murray

Field-Cornet Willie Hofmeyer Louw (30)
Executed by firing squad at Colesberg on 23 November 1901.

Willie Louw came from one of the most respected church-ministerial families in the Paarl area. His father and his three brothers were all ministers of religion. The renowned Reverend AF Louw volunteered to go to St Helena island to be of service to the Boer prisoners banished there. His mother was the sister of the Reverend Andrew Murray, the

Willie Louw of Achtertang, Colesberg.
Source: War Museum of the Boer
Republics

fiery Scottish *dominee* who associated himself entirely with the Boer cause.

It was because of his relationship with Murray that biting remarks were made about Louw and other condemned rebels. During the summing-up at his trial, the chairman of the Military Court described Willie Louw as: 'A rebel of the worst type whose sole object was to attempt to overthrow the Government'[1] and British officers referred to him as 'The brood of Andrew Murray'.[2]

These offensive tirades must be

96

viewed in the light of the attitudes of Milner and the military authorities towards Dutch ministers in the Cape Colony.

In every town there were Dutch ministers and elders who were labelled as 'undesirables'. Many were arrested, charged with high treason, removed from their parishes and interned at Port Alfred.[3] We have already seen how the British commandant of Cradock spoke to the Reverend Reyneke after the execution of Coetzee, saying: 'The blood of Coetzee will be claimed from you and and all the other Dutch ministers'.[4] Reverend Reyneke was an associate of Andrew Murray.

Among many notable persons charged with high treason and interned were the following Church leaders: Professor Lion-Cachet and Reverend Louis Vorster of Burgersdorp, Reverend David Ross of Lady Grey, Reverend Alheit of Ceres, Reverend Wilcocks of Vryburg, Reverend Perold of Warrenton and Reverend Ackerman of Boetsap. Many were placed under house arrest or interned in Port Alfred, among others Reverend Scholtz of Colesberg, Reverend Radloff of Pearston and Reverend Weich of Nieu-Bethesda. In Cradock Reverend Reyneke was forbidden to hold church services. The Officer in Charge of Somerset East locked 45 Afrikaners in the church for days on end. The church in Cradock was at one stage used as a fort. At the execution of Schoeman in Tarkastad, the Catholic priest, Father McCann, was obliged to be in attendance.[5] There are many other examples of this sort of treatment.

In general the Dutch ministers distanced themselves from the conflict and tried to remain neutral. They warned against using force as this was against the Bible, but would not condemn the men captured. It was because of this stance that the most prominent of them, Reverend Andrew Murray, clashed with Milner. He stated that the Church would not openly condemn the uprising of rebels because of the oppression of the Afrikaners by England, and that he could not persuade the rebels otherwise unless the independence of the Republics was guaranteed.[6]

Notwithstanding the implications, the Dutch ministers were quite prepared to visit the condemned, to give comfort and console the unfortunate Boers sentenced to death. They spent the last hours with them and accompanied them along the path to the scaffold or firing squad.

The execution of Willie Louw caused great dismay in church circles. His trial was so unreasonable and unfair that Ramsay MacDonald, a future prime minister of England, said: 'Willie Louw has been shot upon the verdict of a court which did not understand the first elements of justice and had not the faintest idea when a statement was proved'.[7]

When the Boer commandoes invaded the Cape Colony in November 1899 Louw was farming at Agtertang in the Colesberg district. He was called up by General Schoeman to join the Republican forces.[8] To clarify his position he went into the Free State to seek advice from Judge Stuart. His main concern was that whether the Free State had the right to compel colonials to take up arms. He was advised that the Free State had, in fact, annexed sections of the Cape Colony and was entitled to commandeer men. With the second invasion by the Boer commandos of his area, he joined the forces of Commandant Lategan.

On 21 September 1901 Field-Cornet Louw and his burgers were relentlessly pursued by a British column near Philipstown. They were compelled to retreat on foot as their horses were exhausted and could go no further. With six men, he hid on the farm Wolwekuil, but was betrayed by one Jacob du Plessis and taken prisoner.[9] Among those captured was Nicolaas van Wijk who was also to die before a firing squad. Louw was tried before a Military Court on 4 November at Graaff-Reinet, the charges against him including high treason, murder, pillaging and the theft of sheep.

Louw pleaded guilty to the charge of high treason. In his defence he stated that he had acted upon the advice received from Judge Stuart who maintained that he was a Free State citizen. This plea was dismissed by the Military Court. On the charge of the 'murder' of two British soldiers, he told the Court that he was under the command of Commandant Lategan at the skirmish at Damplaas and did not murder the soldiers. This plea was also dismissed.

A further charge of murder arose from the death of a black spy who was working for the British. The evidence in this instance rested solely on information gleaned from one Venter, a member of the commando that had recently surrendered. He stated that the spy had been shot by Piet Bester upon orders from Louw. (Bester was a deserter from the Cape Police and was summarily executed at Marsh Hill near Dordrecht on 18 November 1901.) A British soldier who had been captured by the Boers could not confirm the involvement of Louw at the scene. The defence gave notice that on the day in question Louw was in fact elsewhere with Commandant Lategan.

On the charge of stealing sheep the owner, Van der Linde, testified that Louw had given him a receipt for the sheep as well as fodder. He was unable to say who had slaughtered the sheep. Louw confirmed that Lategan was present when they took the sheep. This plea was also dismissed. It appears that these charges were irrelevant because the accused had already pleaded guilty to high treason. This pretence of a trial generated a guilty verdict and the death penalty.

After the trial Louw was transferred to the Colesberg gaol, where his sister, Mrs M Reyneke of the farm Eenzaamheid, was allowed to visit him twice a week for half an hour. Below is an extract from a letter she wrote to friends.

Eenzaamheid, 9 January 1902

Dear Friends,
As I could not tell you all personally about the passing of my dear brother Willie Louw I thought I should write to you. Would you please pass the letter on to other concerned people.

On three occasions I had the privilege of visiting him for half an hour at a time. On Saturday the 23rd of November (the day of his execution) Mina, Andries and myself

Willie Louw is sentenced to death on the market square in Colesberg.
Source: War Museum of the Boer Republics

visited him at the gaol. He was pleased to see us all and said it was a pity Johan could not be with us as well. He let Mina sit on his knee and Andries beside him ...

This is how we talked until the half-hour expired and the guard notified us that we should leave. Willie stood up immediately and said: 'Now, Sister, we must bid farewell to each other'. I wanted to ignore the word 'farewell' and answered: 'No, Willie, let's just say until we meet again, because I will be here on Monday'. He did not answer me, but took his leave of Mina and Andries. He kissed us all tenderly without saying anything. He then handed me his drinking mug that he used while on commando and asked me to give it to Johan as a keepsake.

When we reached the house in town we heard that a sentence would be proclaimed at half past eleven on the market square. As we did not know who would be sentenced we all stood on the verandah to see who it could be. After a while we saw the procession coming from the gaol.

And there was our darling Willie! Oh, he was so handsome and strong! After a short while the procession returned. Oh, what happened in those few moments? Willie walked back with a steady step and the radiance of health beamed from his face. He was neither pale nor afraid ...

Reverend Reyneke also went to the market square to hear what the sentence would be. When he entered I noticed that he was very pale but calm and could read the outcome on his face. Words were not necessary ...

The sentence would be carried out at three o'clock ...

At about two o'clock Rev. Reyneke and myself went to Willie to be with him to

Willie Louw and Captain Holden at the prison in Colesberg on the day before his execution.
Source: War Museum of the Boer Republics

the end. When we arrived at his cell he was busy gathering all the small articles he used and placed them on a tray. When he was finished with the last task his hands would perform he bent forward slightly so that I could put my arms around his neck. He rested his forehead on my shoulder and said: 'Although I enter the valley of the shadow of death, I shall fear no evil, for Thy rod and Thy staff they comfort me.' He was not concerned about himself but was extremely worried about those that would be left behind. In an emotional voice he said: 'Poor Daddy and Mommy and all of you. And Oh, of poor George I cannot think, poor George! It will be so hard for those left behind, but not for me ...'

He left his Bible for his mother and requested us to advise her that he had written to her. He then gave us farewell greetings for his loved ones. He mentioned them all by name and when he came to Abraham he said: 'You must pray for him because of the wonderful work he is doing on St Helena.'

He asked us to tell George that when the fruit ripens he should take a basket and give it to the prison guards who had looked after him. And so we had the privilege of seeing our dearest brother depart on the short journey to his everlasting home.

The morning had dawned bright and clear. At about midday clouds gathered and by two o'clock we had a strong wind. It was stormy and a few drops of rain fell. At the precise moment that the shots were fired to exchange life for eternity we heard a heavy rumble of thunder. The sun became covered in clouds for the rest of the day, as if nature itself was showing its sympathy.

The following morning, which was Sunday, the sun shone in all its glory ...

M Reyneke

On 23 November, Louw was notified that he would be executed on the same day. He then wrote a short letter to his parents:

Saturday 23/11/1901

My dearest Mother,
I am returning your last letter to you because I am departing to a better world where there is no grief and sorrow. It is stipulated that I will depart this afternoon. It is God's sacred will. He cannot make mistakes. May He always be close to you and dearest Daddy and all our loved ones. May He strengthen you all. Yes, God has promised me that he will strengthen you all, now there is nothing, virtually nothing, that worries me or will hold me back. Oh, I wish I could have done more work for Him. What value there is in a single soul. God, our Father, has allowed it all for the glory and honour of His name. Adieu! Until we meet again my own, dearest Mother.

Willie

A few days later the following death notice appeared in *Ons Land*.

On Saturday afternoon the 23rd of November our dear 'WILLIE' was released from captivity at Colesberg. We who are left behind will have sweet comfort until we meet again.

AA Louw
J Louw
Avondrust, Paarl, 26 November 1901

Willie Louw was executed by firing squad near the animal pound outside Colesberg on the Philippolis road. Although sentenced to death by hanging, this was not possible as no gallows were available in Colesberg. Leading members of the public were 'invited' to attend the execution in spite of the undertaking given after many protests against public execution that this barbaric practice would be ended. Mrs Reyneke suffered so much from these happenings that she died a few months after the death of her brother. She was buried at Eenzaamheid and Willie was later reburied next to her, nearby his parents' graves. His name appears on the Burger Monument in Colesberg.

Willie Louw's grave at Eenzaamheid, Colesberg.
Photograph: Graham Jooste

CHAPTER 13

Active
in Arms

The charge sheets of all the rebels who were captured and brought to trial stated that they were 'active in arms'. This meant that they had committed high treason and were thus liable for the death sentence. The death sentence was generally passed on those who held a particular rank in the commando structure or who were deemed to be influential. Other factors which could mean life or death for the accused were being found guilty of murder, attempted murder, train robbery, arson theft or assault. It was as easy to find aggravating circumstances as it was necessary to make an example of a rebel. Opportunities for 'loading the charges' were numerous and exploited to the full by the Military Courts.

Yet there were instances when 'active in arms' was the only charge that could be laid against certain of the accused. The subsequent executions of these men were heavily condemned by the *Morning Leader*, a British newspaper, which maintained that the actions of the authorities were totally indefensible unless all captured rebels received the death sentence. The Cape law department was also highly critical of the executions of rank-and-file rebels and maintained that an adequate sentence would be one of the loss of all civil rights for five years, including the franchise.[1]

Towards the end of 1901 most of the rebel leaders were behind bars or in their graves. Rebels were executed under the most dubious of circumstances and it can be assumed they were exploited for political reasons as justice did not have a bearing on their sentences at all.

An example of an execution that cried out to the heavens was when Pieter van Heerden, a farmer from Vaalvlei in the Tarkastad district, was executed.

Pieter Willem van Heerden (42)[2]
Executed by firing squad at Tarkastad on 12 November 1901.

Pieter van Heerden was not a rebel. He was unarmed and never went on commando. His charge sheet described him as 'a farmer civilian from Vaalvlei, Tarkastad'. This middle-aged farmer had such bad eyesight that without the aid of his spectacles he could not see ten paces in front of him. Furthermore, without his spectacles he was unable to recognise people in a room. He was also 'so heavy of frame that he could be of no assistance to friend or foe'. He was totally unsuitable for military service.

What possibly riled the authorities was the fact that his son was on commando and had distinguished himself by capturing five British troopers while alone and unarmed. What also may have counted heavily

Pieter van Heerden of Vaalvlei, Tarkastad.
Source: Hoe Zij Sterven

against him was the humiliating defeat the 17th Lancers suffered at the hand of General Smuts and his commando in the Tarkastad district. After this setback on 17 September the military issued a strongly worded proclamation to the inhabitants of Tarkastad. During this period the helpless Van Heerden was languishing in a cell at the gaol on a minor charge. He was the only scapegoat available.

Van Heerden was taken into custody by the 17th Lancers on 9 August 1901 at his farm Vaalvlei. He was interned in Steynsburg gaol for two months without any charges being

104

brought against him. A month after the defeat of the Lancers at Elands River Pass he was transferred to Graaff-Reinet to face trial by a Military Court consisting of Lieutenant-Colonel W Doran (Royal Irish Rifles), Major RJ Mullins (Dragoon Guards and Brabants Horse) and Lieutenant TP Dawson (PAGMI). The prosecutor was Captain Sandys Lumsdaine (HLI) and the interpreter Sergeant Peters.* After being found guilty he was sent back to Steynsburg without knowing what fate awaited him. A month later he was taken to Tarkastad and executed.

During this period, several British soldiers lost their lives in skirmishes with the Smuts commando, clad in khaki taken from the 17th Lancers. Five burgers were executed in various districts for wearing British uniforms. On 12 November, Tarkastad was shocked by the execution of this harmless, half-blind man. Once more, an atrocious sentence robbed a family of a dear one.

On 6 August a Boer commando arrived at his farm, followed the next day by a British patrol. Van Heerden testified that the patrol requested slaughter sheep and warned him not to leave his house. They told him that they had placed sentries in the veld. They returned the following day and searched the house. Shortly after their departure a skirmish with the Boers took place.

A British officer testified that at about 1000 yards from the farmhouse they were fired upon by the Boers. Nobody was killed but some of his men were taken prisoner. Furthermore he stated that shots were fired from the direction of the house.

Van Heerden acknowledged that the Boers were at his house and had fetched him after the skirmish. They took him to their camp but then sent him back to his house and told him to remain there until they had left the farm. He and his wife watched as the commando rode away with their captives.

Two black spies were the key witnesses. The first one testified that he had been spying on Van Heerden's house and was later ordered by the officer to go to the house. He maintained that as he was approaching the house he was fired upon. However, he was unable to state that it was Van Heerden who fired the shot. The second witness testified that he could not confirm that Van Heerden was among the Boers.

* Attorney-General File AG 3560, 3636, Blue Book Ref 44, M121, Cape Archives.

Van Heerden was not arrested immediately. The following day he received a message from a British officer ordering him and his neighbour, Venter, to come to the camp. It was on Venter's farm that the skirmish had taken place. They were then both arrested and taken to Steynsburg. Venter was later released but Van Heerden was kept in captivity for more than three months and then executed. During his final internment in Tarkastad, his wife and children rented a small house so that they could visit him in gaol. This was an agonising period for them as they had to apply to the military authorities for permission to visit him and were never sure if their request would be granted. When it was, they were escorted by armed guards to and from the cells.

As was customary, certain people were issued with orders to be present at the proclamation of sentence in Tarkastad. The sentence left the inhabitants stunned, as most people were of the opinion that because of his physical disability and bad eyesight he could of been of little assistance to the Boers. The commanding officer announced loudly: 'That he had recently joined the enemy, that he had taken up arms against the lawful Government and had attempted murder. The accusations are punishable by hanging but instead of that he will be shot.' The last certainly because of his great weight.

That the case against Van Heerden was weak is indicated by the following document, which appears in the records at the Attorney-General's Office in Cape Town, which states: 'The case is weak in that there is nothing to show whether he had been with them (the Boers) any length of time, or was a man of position, or why in fact he should have suffered the death penalty. This Legal Department would have classified him as rank and file [Class II rebel, punishable by loss of franchise for five years].

A more damning comment regarding a court's administration of reasonable and fair justice will not easily be found. And yet the sentence was ratified by Kitchener!

Before his execution, Van Heerden was visited by a Mr LJ van Heerden, who had heard that during his three months of incarceration he was not allowed to speak to an attorney. Furthermore, he was not allowed to call witnesses on his behalf. Because his wife could not receive permission to visit him again, he had sent her a message saying

Pieter van Heerden of Tarkastad seated in his chair just before being executed by firing squad in front of 'undesirable' inhabitants, while two bags of quicklime lie in readiness next to his open grave. An English minister in white stands behind the convicted man.
Source: Steynsburg Museum

that she should be seated at the feet of the Lord, from where she would receive strength and comfort.

His friend accompanied him along the Skaapkraal road leading from Tarkastad. Because of his size he had to be helped on and off the ambulance wagon. When they arrived at the place of execution a large grave had already been dug. After he was tied to a chair, his friend read him a short passage from the Bible, which he repeated word for word. Ten soldiers stood in readiness and waited for the command to fire.

As the blood gushed from his mouth, a coloured labourer mockingly said: 'But listen! The Boer has blood!'

The medical report read as follows:

The commandant
TARKASTAD

I attended the execution of Pieter Willem van Heerden at the place of execution who was condemned to death and was shot at 7 am on the 12th of November 1901.

On making my post mortem examination I found death to be due to gunshot wounds. Four shots in the head and face were sufficient to cause him death. Three wounds in the thorax were through the heart and would have caused instant death. Two wounds in the abdomen would not have been necessarily fatal.

Tarkastad
12/11/1901
A Taylor Brown
Medical Officer i/c Troops.

The following appeared in the *Graaff-Reinet Advertiser* a few days later:

EXECUTION AT TARKASTAD

On Monday afternoon a parade of the Town Guard and Royal Fusileers was ordered in front of the Commandant's office to hear sentence of death on Piet Willem van Heerden from Vaalvlei.

Convicted of attempted murder and tried at Graaff-Reinet, the sentence was carried out at 6.30 am on Tuesday morning. Present were the Commandant, the Town Guard and the Royal Fusileers.

Neither of the local Ministers being in town, a Catholic Priest, Father McCann remained with the condemned man and was present at the execution by firing squad. The execution took place a distance out of town on the Skaapkraal road.

Mr LJ van Heerden read appropriate prayers and at a signal from the Commandant a volley was fired. Death was instantaneous. The deceased leaves a widow and family to which much sympathy is felt.

The devilish manner whereupon this sentence was carried out is most certainly unique in the history of civilised nations.[3]

The dramatic photograph of this execution by firing squad was taken by an unknown person and is to be found in the Steynsburg Museum. After the war, Van Heerden's son Gustavus received the necessary permission and reburied his father in the Tarkastad cemetery. His headstone simply says:

Pieter Willem van Heerden
Born 27 Oct 1859
Died 12 Nov 1901

Pieter van Heerden's grave in the cemetery at Tarkastad.
Photograph: Graham Jooste

Nicolaas Francois van Wijk (26)[4]
Executed by firing squad at Colesberg on 12 November 1901.

Captured with Willie Louw at Kareepoort near Philipstown, Van Wijk was tried by Military Court at Graaff-Reinet on 2 October 1901. Besides the charge of 'active in arms', he was also accused of 'disgraceful conduct of a cruel kind.'

During cross-examination, he acknowledged that he was born in the Cape Colony but had moved to the Transvaal a year before the war broke out, where he saw service with the commando sent out against Magato. He took the oath of allegiance and became a burger of the Transvaal, then joined the Transvaal Police (Zarps) and was stationed in the Soutpansberg area. With the outbreak of hostilities he was called up for duty.

Van Wijk conducted his own defence and asked for permission to get his documents from Middelburg, Transvaal, but was sentenced to death the same day! According to a report in the *Graaff-Reinet Advertiser,* there was no investigation done to establish his credentials. The onus was on him to convince the court of such but there had been no time. He was executed as a Cape rebel although everything pointed to his citizenship of the Transvaal.

The incident that led to the execution of Van Wijk took place in a small settlement called Vanwyksvlei in the Karoo. A small detail of Boers rode into the town with the idea of disrupting communications. They approached the post office and demanded the keys. At the trial a Miss Walton testified that she would not hand them over, and stood with her back against the door.

She was pushed aside and her raincoat torn, roughly handled by various Boers and one had tried to kiss her. The post office was then burned down and Van Wijk did nothing to stop the fire.

Van Wijk was found guilty on all charges and transferred to Colesberg where he was executed some 10 days before Louw. The court report stated: 'It is not clear whether the accused was a burger of the Transvaal. The case is weak on this point.'[5]

Proclamation of sentence was heard on the market square at Colesberg on 11 November. Van Wijk was sentenced to be hanged but was instead executed by firing squad along the Hanover road leading from the town. A short while before his execution he wrote the following letter to his family:

Colesberg Prison
12 November 1901

My Dearest Father, Mother, Brothers and Sisters,
By the grace of God I now have the opportunity to write to you for the last time. Oh! do not be upset about what I am going to write. The Lord God of Heaven help you. Nothing happens without His will. Upon His will I have placed myself and I am satisfied what He has prepared for me. Today I was sentenced to death. My Parents, I am prepared for death, not because of felony, but because of false witnesses. I forgive those who gave evidence against me. May the Lord also forgive them.

Father, I am sending you my pocket watch and chain to be worn in memory of me. For Mother I am sending two pounds and to Annie my ring and to Dollie a brooch. I am returning your photographs. I am sending these with the Rev. Hofmeyr from Hanover who has been with me for a short while. He spoke to me and has shown me the way to the Lord.

Parents, Brothers, and Sisters, do not be worried about me. We will all meet again hereafter. Write to Johanna for me. Keep the Lord before your eyes, because we never know when we will have to leave this Earth.

I now kiss you all with sincerity. Your eternally abandoned son. May God be merciful towards me.

N van Wijk

The name of N van Wijk appears on the Burger Monument at Colesberg. No photograph can be found of this young man who was executed under such questionable circumstances. His grave is unknown.

Johannes Hermanus Roux (18)[6]
Executed by firing squad at Graaff-Reinet on 7 October 1901.

This handsome and reserved young man joined up with a commando at the age of 17. He was captured on his 18th birthday during a sharp skirmish far from home.

Roux was from the farm Jordaanskraal in the Grahamstown area and was taken prisoner at Ventershoek in the Steynsburg district on 8 August 1901. Roux and four other commandos sought shelter in a donga and allegedly fired upon British soldiers from there. When Roux realised that their shelter had been discovered, he raised his hands and surrendered to Lieutenant Barber. It is not known what happened to the other Boers, but fate had caught up with him.

Apart from being accused of being 'active in arms', he was charged with the 'attempted murder' of Lieutenant Barber, tried by the Military Court at Graaff-Reinet on 30 August and sentenced to death.

*Attorney-General's File AG 3636, 3560, Blue Book 45, M62. Cape Archives.

The stunned 18-year-old Johannes Roux listens to his death sentence on the market square
of Graaff-Reinet.
Source: Die Afrikaner en sy kultuur, *by Grobbelaar and Strydom*

The Reverend Charles Murray visited Roux in his prison cell and was greatly impressed by the youngster's attitude: 'He was calm, but something in his eyes portrayed dignity, nobility and maturity. During his execution he was humble, though brave.'

Asked by Murray if he was ready to meet his God, he answered immediately: 'No, Sir, I am not prepared to die.' Murray explained that although his past life was not that of a 'boisterous and excessive sinner' it did not entitle him to salvation by God. He had to repent his sins. That night this little verse came into Roux's mind:

'I confess my sins to Jesus,

The purest lamb of God ...'

And so, according to Murray, Johannes Roux received forgiveness for his sins and entered willingly into the valley of death.

Murray accompanied him to the place of execution, where he requested that a letter be written for him to his parents explaining that he was at peace and entered eternity with joy in his heart.

They prayed together at the open grave and he delivered himself to

God. He wrote the following letter to his mother from his death cell:

Graaff-Reinet, 6 October 1901

Loving Mother!
I am taking this opportunity to write a few lines to you to advise that I am going to my Fatherland. I have been tried and sentenced to death. So, my dear Mother, you must not despair over me. I am safe with the Lord. Oh, my dear Mother, how I longed for you, but I will be patient with what lies ahead for me. I will never see you again on this Earth. All of you must try to meet your God.

I end this with best greetings to you all. I remain your son.

Johannes Hermanus Roux.

Johannes Roux of Jordaanskraal, Grahamstown.
Source: Hoe Zij Sterven

Along the Spandau Mountain road outside Graaff-Reinet, the young Roux died before the firing squad. His name appears on the Boer Memorial in Graaff-Reinet, along with all the others executed near this town. In 1908 his remains were transferred to a communal grave together with the six other burgers who were executed. Their names do not appear on the monument in the cemetery.

Jacobus Francois Geldenhuys (25)[7]
Executed by firing squad at Graaff-Reinet on 14 February 1902.

Geldenhuys, from Vlakplaas in the Graaff-Reinet district, was captured at Driefontein near Nieu-Bethesda on 20 December 1901. He was accused of firing upon and wounding two British troopers in a skirmish at Martinshof five months previously, and also of the theft of clothing and food. He was tried by Military Court in Graaff-Reinet on 18 January 1902 and condemned to death.

The sentence came as a shock to him and Reverend Murray found

113

him in tears in his cell. While awaiting sentence, he wrote the following verse:

'The Lord is my Saviour and my light,
Whom shall I fear?
The Lord is the strength of my life,
From whom shall I take fright?'

The night before his execution, he wrote a letter to his family:

Graaff-Reinet, 13/2/1902

Dear Brother and Sister,
A sad message I must make known to you, and that is that I have been sentenced to death.

Do not be sorrowful. The Lord will do what is right for me. I will wait for you with my mother and sister in heaven. I die for my blood. Jesus died for me. I want Him by my side. I cast myself desperately into His arms.

Dear Brother and Sister, do what you like with my belongings. I will also send my blanket. Please give it to Sannie. I send my fondest love to her.

I remain your separated but expectant brother and send love and my blessings to you all.

Jacobus F Geldenhuys

In 1908 his remains were reburied, together with the other executed Boers, in the old cemetery at Graaff-Reinet. His name appears on the Burger Monument in Graaff-Reinet.

CHAPTER 14

Two Fighters and a Traitor

Deserters from the British Army who joined the Boer forces and were captured were immediately executed as traitors. Any British citizen who aided the Boers or fought for them was classified as a rebel. Coloured people who spied for the Boers were executed.

When a Boer deserter who joined the British forces was caught and executed by the Boers, it was murder and the 'joiner' became a British martyr. Likewise, when the Boers caught and executed a black spy, it was also classified as murder.

This was the measure by which the victor meted out justice.

Lieutenant Piet Bester[1]

Executed by firing squad at Marsh Hill, Dordrecht, on 24 November 1901.

This intrepid and fierce police deserter who threw his lot in with the Boers became a legend in his lifetime. He feared nothing, least of all for his own life. The British called him a scoundrel and a bandit, but to the Boers he was a hero.

When the Boers invaded the Cape for a second time, Piet Bester deserted his post at Burgersdorp and joined a commando. His police rank was that of Lieutenant. Bester served under Commandant HW Lategan in the Steynsburg region. His name was mentioned in the trial of Field-Cornet Willie Louw as the person who shot a black spy on Louw's orders.[2]

On 2 June 1901 the small town of Jamestown was captured by General PH Kritzinger, whose commando replenished itself with arms, ammunition and provisions. Later in the day Bester rode in with his small band of daredevils and promptly set about plundering the armoury, shops and the hotel. Bester's small commando consisted of about 20 horsemen, who supported themselves by ambushing and looting British provision wagons. After the occupation of Jamestown, Bester dug in and prevented any stores and post from reaching the beleagured town for four months. Transport to Aliwal North was also affected and the delivery of goods became erratic and uncertain. During this occupation, a British historian declared the town to be 'the capital of the Orange Free State'.[3]

The memorial column at Dordrecht on the mass grave where Piet Bester and three others burgers were reinterred.
Photograph: Abrie Oosthuizen

Bester occasionally joined up with the commandos of Fouchee or Myburgh, but always broke away again with his men to operate on their own in the Stormberg area. Fouchee once took a *sjambok* to Bester over an indescretion committed. After that he operated along with Myburgh on a few occasions. The daring and fearlessness of Bester's looting sorties made him renowned throughout the Stormberg region.

On 16 November 1901 he became another victim of that brilliant 'rebel hunter' Colonel Harry Scobell and his men. Bester's hideout at Koningskroon was discovered and reported by a betrayer. Some of Myburgh's men were also captured, together with Bester himself and 20 rebels. Among those captured was one Steenberg, who turned Crown witness in the case of Lieutenant Izak Liebenberg. For this act he secured his freedom.

Bester was taken to a British camp at

Marsh Hill in the Dordrecht district, tried before a Military Court and summarily executed. The British wanted a public execution and approached a house that served as a clinic for pregnant women that was run by a midwife of renown. They totally misjudged the character of Mrs Coetzer who flew into the soldiers and chased them away, berating them for their planned horrible deed in front of pregnant women.

According to the British officer in charge, Bester refused to be blindfolded and requested to be shot from the front. Bester also told the officer that he did not blame him because if he had caught the officer he would have shot him. The officer complied with Bester's request and removed the blindfold. The firing squad then refused to shoot as they would be looking into the eyes of a condemned man. He was then turned around and eight shots hit him simultaneously between the shoulderblades. As he lived, so he died. The British officer later declared that Bester was the bravest man he had ever come across.

Bester was buried in a shallow grave. A family member visited the grave after the war and was astonished to see a hand protruding from it. She had a deeper grave dug and erected stones over it. This grave was a well-known beacon in the district until the remains were eventually interred in the Dordrecht cemetery.

The name of Bester appears on a mass grave in the Dordrecht cemetery as well as on a memorial in the Heroes' Acre at the Dutch Reformed Church in the town. Seventeen other burgers who lost their lives in the vicinity are commemorated here as well. The inscription reads:

'Heroes to the last drop of blood,
Undaunted, fearless, brave, loyal and good.'

There is no photograph of Piet Bester.

Francois Edward Davis (30)[4]
Executed by firing squad at Somerset East on 25 January 1902.

Before sunrise on the morning of 25 January 1902 a large crowd gathered at a small drift on the banks of the Bosch River, on the road to Pearston and a short distance from Somerset East. On the bank was an open grave with a chair beside it and two bags of unslaked lime.

At 6 am, an ambulance wagon drawn by two mules approached the

Francois Davis of the district of Bedford.
Source: Hoe Zij Sterven

place of execution. Fourteen soldiers of the Royal Fusileers took up their positions at 25 paces from the grave. The approaching wagon became bogged down in a pool of mud and the clumsy drivers could not shift it. After a while Davis himself said to them: 'Give me the reins, I am a good driver'. The soldiers did not respond and after a great struggle the wagon proceeded towards the grave. Davis stepped off the wagon and walked purposefully towards it. He stood for a moment and peered into the grave, then turned and sat down on the chair. The gruesome ritual was about to begin. A rope was bound around his body and arms and tied at the back of the chair. His feet were tied to the legs of the chair. A blindfold covered his eyes. The firing squad was at the ready – all picked marksmen. None of them knew who had drawn blank or live cartridges. As Davis lifted his head, the order was shouted and the volley thudded into him. The unfortunate man toppled into the grave and a sigh was heard from the spectators. The legs of the chair stuck out above the grave. Dr Legge examined the body and pronounced him dead. The slaked lime was poured over the body and it was covered with soil. The silent spectators drifted away, still shocked.

That is how Francois Davis, a deserter from Nesbitt's Horse, met his death – just like a rebel.

The likeable 30-year-old Davis was originally from the Bedford district in the Eastern Cape. It appears that he joined the Dutch Reformed Church as a result of a visit by Reverend Steyn just before his execution. His family was Afrikaans-speaking and letters demonstrate that he stood firmly behind the Afrikaner cause.

Davis had previously been a member of Nesbitt's Horse, an Eastern Cape regiment formed by colonial troops in 1899. He attached himself to a Boer commando at Struishoek in the Somerset East district in March

1901. They then proceeded to the Free State. On 15 October he was captured with four of his comrades on a farm in the Wepener district.

From his cell he wrote this moving letter to his family the night before his execution. He had as yet not heard what his sentence would be.

Somerset East (Prison)
22 January 1901

Dear Brothers and Sisters
As my time is short upon this Earth it is my desire to see my wife and child once more. Brother Jan, please be kind enough to send my wife to me to say farewell as I know my time is very short ...

Brothers and Sisters, I am now prepared to die and I am not afraid. God is with me and I am reconciled with Him. My only plea is to see my wife again. I am prepared to meet my death. I know I have to die. Bring my wife and child, I want to greet them, that is my only desire. I know I am to die and am ready for my sentence. The sooner I am with Jesus the better it will be for me.

My Brothers, if I cannot see my wife, give her my greetings and ask her to greet my child for me on our farm and to rear her well. God wants all the little children.

But Brothers, bring my wife to me as I have something to say to her. The brooch is for her as it is my handiwork. I made it from a small stone while I was in captivity. Preserve it for our child as a souvenir of her father. My pipe, knife and two sleeve buttons should be divided among you in memory of your brother.

God is my guide, I will lack nothing. Goodbye, my dear Brothers and Sisters. I wish you could all be as happy as I am to die in the arms of the Lord. God knows me and has accepted me.

I desire to be with the Lord. Use His word and do not forget His path. This war was meant to forge us not only into a nation of the world but also a nation of God. Read Psalm 146 and Isaiah 41 verse 10.

Greetings from your brother. God be with you all.

Francois Edward Davis

His brothers responded to his plea and his wife and daughter arrived that Friday morning in Somerset East, the day before his execution. They had to obtain permission from the town commandant to visit the gaol. She mentioned how frightened she was that he might receive the death sentence, but he answered her: 'Jesus was hanged and I am no better than He. He was crucified for me, and I will die for our nation.'

He then took his little daughter into his arms and said: 'Yes, my child, my regret is that I will not be able to rear you. I would have taught you to search for the Lord in your early life. There is nothing more beautiful than to be seen as a child of God'.

He went on to tell his wife about a wonderful experience he had had during the night: 'At about midnight last night my cell became aglow with light. At first I thought it was somebody with a lantern! Beside me I saw an angel in white and with the wings of a dove. Before I could speak I was told that I would be condemned to death and that I should prepare myself. Hereafter it was as if I was in a trance.' They then had to part, and his wife promised to visit him after he had been sentenced. He took his little girl into his arms once more and asked his wife not to bring her to see him again.

Davis and a burger from Lötter's commando received their proclamations on the market square that same day. One was to live and the other to die. His beloved wife and Reverend Steyn from Bedford were allowed to visit him for the last time. The child was not with them.

Eight days after the execution, a heavy thunderstorm partly washed away Davis' grave. The leg of the chair as well as his foot protruded above the soil. The grave was opened and repaired and the chair burnt. The screws from the burnt chair were saved and sent to his widow with the following message: 'Accept these screws as a souvenir. Show them to the other Boers who do not honour their King. Tell them that they will also be shot if they do not surrender.'

In spite of the request lodged with Kitchener six months previously to abandon public executions, many 'volunteers' were reported to have been present. The Somerset East *Budget* requested that the Government identify the grave and place the reason for the execution upon it. This would serve as a reminder to those fanning the flames of rebellion that the crime of taking up arms illegally would be paid for as in this case.

The whereabouts of Davis's grave are unknown and no monument is to be found for him or for Claassen, who was also executed in Somerset East. The only object upon which their names appear is a walking stick in the Somerset East museum carved by a Boer prisoner in Port Alfred.

Lieutenant Izak Bartholomeus Liebenberg (18)[5]
Executed by hanging at Aliwal North on 11 January 1902.

The body of Lieutenant Leopold Nieumeyer of the British police in Smithfield was found in a donga between Aliwal North and Rouxville in the Free State. At the autopsy it was pointed out that he had received two gunshot wounds, one in the shoulder from behind and one through the head. A year later, a Boer, Lieutenant Izak Liebenberg of the Scheepers commando, was hanged in Aliwal North for Nieumeyer's murder. The double standards applied in this trial struck out like a sore thumb.

Nieumeyer was born a Free Stater and had grown up in Smithfield. He was resident in Rhodesia for a while before returning to Smithfield to marry, settle down and become accepted as a Free Stater.

After the annexation of the Free State by Britain, Nieumeyer joined the British police and turned against the Boer population. Because of his continual harassment, the Boers had every reason to execute him as a traitor. He was honoured by the British as a soldier who had died for Queen and Country,[6] although he had never renounced his Free State citizenship. As a lieutenant in the 'Orange River Police', he distinguished himself by burning down Boer farmhouses, rounding up their cattle and sheep and sending the women and children to concentration camps. He also hunted down Boers who had broken their oath of neutrality. He was branded by the Boers and they were thirsting for his blood.

When Scheepers and Fouchee started reorganising the southern Free State in preparation for an invasion of the Cape Colony by Boer forces, the order went out to get him. He was to be executed immediately upon capture, and evidently had a reward on his head.

Nieumeyer was on his way to the Aliwal North gaol with a batch of Boer prisoners when he rode into an ambush at Stolzkraal. Next to Nieumeyer on the cart sat another traitor by the name of Van Aswegen, whom Nieumeyer was bringing to Aliwal North for his own safety. During the skirmish, Van Aswegen escaped with a bullet through his hat, but the Boers got their prize, Nieumeyer, who threw his hands into air. Nieumeyer's body was found later, a few miles away. According to a report by Lieutenant Fanie Swanepoel to Commandant Scheepers, he

Lieutenant Izak Liebenberg of Grootfontein, Philippolis, in the Orange Free State.
Source: Hoe Zij Sterven

was shot while trying to escape. Later at least five burgers boasted that they had been responsible of the deed. Others claimed to have heard another shot after Nieumeyer was wounded.

Two key witnesses in the trial were Tobias du Plessis and Frans Steenberg, who became Crown witness in exchange for their freedom. They pointed out Izak Liebenberg as the person to have fired the shot that wounded Nieumeyer. Although the death-shot through the head was evidently triggered by Lieutenant Fanie Swanepoel, who had since been killed in a skirmish near Somerset East with a British patrol, Liebenberg was charged with murder.

Liebenberg was among the 30 Scheeper commando members captured in the Camdeboo on 12 July 1901. Although eight of his confederates had already been executed, he was quickly linked to the death of Nieumeyer and sent to Aliwal North. During his internment the search for witnesses to testify against him was intensified. On 20 November he was charged with 'murder and of being an accessory before the fact to murder'. The Military Court was made up as follows: Colonel Hughes-Hallet of the Seaforth Highlanders, President, Major Garland of the Highland Light Infantry and Captain Earle of the 3rd Lancashire Regiment. Captain CP Halse was the prosecutor and Alleyne Yeld the interpreter.*

It was mainly on the grounds of evidence given by Steenberg and Du Plessis that Liebenberg was found guilty.

In his comprehensive work *Smithfield*, A Prinsloo writes that the execution of Liebenberg was a huge blunder and that 'Tobias du Plessis wandered around Smithfield in isolation like a lost ox apparently because his conscience troubled him'.

In his closing statement, defence lawyer RR Walker dwelt on the contradictory evidence of the Crown witnesses and exposed Du Plessis as totally untrustworthy and unreliable. He went on to prove that despite

---

* *Northern Post and Border News*, Aliwal North, 22 November 1901.

122

the hypocritical stance of the prosecution as regards the 'murder' of Nieumeyer, he was not a British soldier, but in fact a Free State burger who had betrayed his people and would have been found guilty in any court martial conducted by the Boer military. Furthermore, he would have been executed had he not tried to escape. He referred strongly to the case of Piet Bester, who had deserted from the British police and joined the Boers. The British considered him a traitor and had summarily executed him. They made him out to be a villain as well, and that was not deemed 'murder'. In the case of Nieumeyer, here was a man who had betrayed his own people and

Izak Liebenberg (No. 1 in the photograph, seond row, left) photographed in Graaff-Reinet with other prisoners.
Source: War Museum of the Boer Republics

yet the British regarded him as a hero and martyr. Yet the similarity between the two cases was overlooked and the Boers were guilty of 'murder'. 'Why do the Boers not enjoy the privilege of executing a traitor the same as the British have?' cried Walker in indignation.

Reports on the findings of the court as well as the execution of Izak Liebenberg were evidently under censorship and nothing can be found in newspaper reports of that time. Microfilm at the Cape Archives indicates that the appropriate pages in the *Northern Post* of Aliwal North were torn out. Likewise, there is no mention in the neighbouring Barkly East *Reporter* of the trial. This seems sinister, as executions of rebels were usually trumpeted out in detail. Also strange was the fact that proclamation of sentence was not done publicly, but in the backyard of the gaol, contrary to the usual ceremonies held in public to announce the pending death of a rebel.

And so the execution of Izak Liebenberg disappeared from the annals of Aliwal North. As late as 1977, FJ du Plooy wrote in his book *Aliwal North, One Hundred Years* that the court had adjourned without a

A scene on the market square at Aliwal North when 13 rebels were sentenced. Seven of them were sentenced to death, but their sentences were later commuted to life imprisonment. Source: Aliwal Museum

conclusive finding. To this day, few inhabitants of Aliwal North are aware that somebody was executed in their town during the Anglo-Boer War.

Soon after the execution of Liebenberg, seven rebels were sentenced to death at Aliwal North, but were reprieved. One of the condemned was ill and awaited the outcome of his fate in gaol. The proclamation of these sentences was fully covered by the *Northern Post* as a rumour spread that a rebel had been hanged in the gaol. The *Northern Post* responded: 'Of course there is no truth in such matters.'

Liebenberg was hanged in the Aliwal North gaol on Saturday 11 January 1902. In reality, he was hanged 'twice'. This macabre account was detailed in an unpublished manuscript about the war experiences of a 15-year-old rebel, Witkop von Caues, as put down by his son, Leon von Caues. Witkop and a group of teenagers were interned in the gaol at Ailwal North when they were ordered to attend the execution of a prisoner called Liebenberg. 'Early the next morning I was woken up by two men singing *Nearer my God to Thee*. I assumed that it was Izak and the

124

church minister who had been watching over Izak all night. I could not go to sleep again and was worried about what would happen to me and my friends.' At nine o'clock the next morning all the prisoners were standing along the wall of the inner courtyard of the prison. The gallows were already erected on one side of the courtyard. Everything was dead quiet when Izak walked in proudly and upright with a grey cap on his head. He walked directly towards the gallows. He climbed up the steps and paused for a while, turned around, looked at us against the wall and nodded. He then went and stood directly under the rope. A person in khaki with a black hat on approached him and put the rope around his neck. He stood to one side and suddenly pulled the handle. Izak dropped through the trapdoor and at the same time a curtain fell over the gallows. After a few moments, two Khakies stepped forward and pulled the curtain back. There stood Izak ... unscathed! The structure was too low or maybe the Khakies had forgotten to dig a hole under the body because Izak was standing with both feet on the ground! Two Khakies rushed in with some convicts who immediately used their picks and shovels to dig a hole under the trapdoor. While this was going on Izak walked across to the prisoners standing next to the wall, shook hands with them and started talking. The Boers were all dumbstruck and many could not utter a word, but Izak addressed them in a strong voice!

When Izak had greeted the last Boer, he turned around and again walked

Liebenberg's name appears on the Roll of Honour in the
Concentration Camp Memorial Garden at Aliwal North.
Photograph: Abrie Oosthuizen

towards the gallows. He climbed up the steps but when he reached the top one he turned around and his cap fell off and rolled down the steps. He hesitated for a moment and we thought he was going to fetch his cap. He stopped and said: 'Go, my old cap, your master is also going.'

This whole process was re-enacted and when the curtain was withdrawn they saw the body of Izak swaying at the end of the rope. His head was drooping at an angle on his chest. He was dead.

Izak Liebenberg was buried in the old concentration-camp cemetery at Aliwal North. His family later reburied him on the family farm, Grootfontein, in the Philippolis district of the Free State. His mother placed his remains in the grave of his father who had died a year after the war and erected a tombstone over their communal grave.

While Mrs Liebenberg was in the concentration camp at Bethulie, she received a letter from Reverend J du Plessis, informing her of her son's death. A shortened version follows:

Aliwal North, 14th January 1902
Mrs HCW Liebenberg
Norvalspont Camp

Esteemed and tender friend,
It has been my sorrowful plight and duty to cheer up your son during the last hours of his life.

The Lord has called upon you to drink and empty the most bitter chalice. I can merely comfort myself with the words of your son: 'My mother is a Christian. She knows where to seek her comfort. God Himself will give her strength'.

Let me now tell you about his last hours. The sentence was read out by the commandant in the courtyard of the prison. Izak was then taken back to his cell where I immediately joined him. His only request was to see a young lady, Miss Kitty Snijman, from the concentration camp. This I could manage for him ...

Upon a question from me he acknowledged that he had been converted to the Lord about four months ago ... late on Friday night he told me that he had fired a shot at Nieumeyer under orders from his commanding officer. He also mentioned that he had no malice against anyone, including the man who had testified so heavily against him. He would face death without a grudge or hatred against anyone on earth.

On the Saturday morning he was calm and peaceful. He was calmer than I was, because when we started to pray and I thought of his youth and strength I could not control my tears and no words came to my lips. At seven o'clock he said farewell to his fellow captives. It was such a touching scene and again I could not control my tears ... As he mounted the scaffold I read out loudly to him: 'Whosoever hears My word and believes in Me will have everlasting life. The judgement will be of one from death unto life.' A few minutes later he was no more. The prayers that he offered up for his dear mother and father and brothers will certainly be heard. May the Lord grant you His mercy day after day.

Rev. J du Plessis

The night before his execution, Izak had written his last letter:

Aliwal North, 10/1/1902

My Mother and little Brother,
I know how bitter the chalice will be for you when you hear the sad tidings. My dear Mother, you must be satisfied to hear about the sentence of death from your son. You must accept the will of the Lord, however bitter it might be. Mother, the Lord has forgiven me all my sins and I belong to Him. What He does is for the better ...

I wish you all God's richest blessings and also to my little brother and all my friends ... Farewell, my Mother. Now we must part. So, my dearest Mother, do not grieve for me. I am safe with the Lord and what He does is good ...

I have requested Rev. du Plessis to send you all my belongings as well as my portraits. You can then do with them as you please. If only you and my little brother could be with me now. Oh, my Father and my two brothers do not even know what my condition is. If you happen to meet them one day, advise them to seek refuge in the Lord. He will save them.

Mother, all my hope is with the Lord ... I greet you for the last time.

Your son,
Izak Bartholomeus Liebenberg

P.S. Give my watch to my Father, my leggings to Barend, my hat to Alit and my belt to Hennie.
Safe in the arms of Jesus
Gently I fled unto his breast
There in His dearest shadow
My glory and my rest

Years later this letter appeared in *Die Volksblad*:

VAARWEL
The last letter from one convicted

Dear Brother,

Keep this in remembrance from me, your convicted brother who will be hanged tomorrow. He has found his Lord. Be faithful to the Lord and your country. I am going to leave you with a redeemed heart and I wish you all God's richest blessings. Oh! it is bitter. My hours are numbered. I will thank the Lord when the time arrives, but I must await my Redeemer and Saviour.

So, my Brother, think of your God during your young days with a pure heart. You must say: 'From this time forward I want to serve my God and say farewell to all worldly company and idleness. From now on I want to be a Christian'. Oh! Brother! Believe that completely and you will never be in fear of death or hell.

Farewell, my dearest young Brother! Farewell! My Father is calling me: Come! Keep this letter as a memory of your never to be forgotten Brother.

IB Liebenberg
Born 8 July 1883
Executed 11 January 1902 at 4 o'clock
Farewell!

The grave at Grootfontein, Philippolis,
where Izak Liebenberg was reinterred
with his father.
Photograph: Graham Jooste

CHAPTER 15

Executions of
Coloured People

On the charge sheets of eight rebels who were condemned to death, the main allegations were murder of coloured people who spied or fought for the British. The charge also held good for those who fought against the Coloured Corps, who were armed by the British. The condemned were:

- PJ Fourie: For the execution of a coloured spy in the Cape Midlands. (Chapter 7)
- Commandant JC Lötter: For the execution of two coloured spies in the Cape Midlands. (Chapter 10)
- Field-Cornet W Louw: For the execution of a coloured spy in the Colesberg district. (Chapter 12)
- AC Jooste and HL Jacobs: Took part in action against a coloured column, the Border Scouts, in the Kenhardt district. (Chapter 16)
- A Renike and L Brink: The shooting of two Scouts during the siege of Mafeking. (Chapter 17)
- Hermanus and Johannes Kuhn: The shooting of Scouts during a skirmish in the Vryburg district. (Chapter 18)
- Commandant Gideon Scheepers: The execution of seven coloured spies in the Cape Midlands. (Chapter 19)
- Commandant Edwin Conroy: Who would have been convicted on 71 charges of murder of Border Scouts if he had been captured. He fled to South-West Africa and then to Europe. (Chapter 16)

The executions of burgers for the above 'murders' was one of the most controversial issues of the day. These took place during the guerilla-warfare stage of the conflict and warrant closer scrutiny.

Although the use of coloured or black soldiers was not in conflict with international law, both parties originally refrained from arming them, by tacit agreement. They were however used as drivers, scouts and for general support behind the lines.[1]

The attitude of Britain was that no black or coloured men would be needed in the pending conflict as it would be over before Christmas. Also, the social structures of both parties and their attitudes towards non-white combatants placed them in similar positions. Thus in the beginning it was purely a 'white man's war' and the use of blacks would be avoided.[2]

In England, public opinion was similar, because of the cultural differences between the races. One newspaper stated: 'There was the danger of their getting out of hand and committing the attrocities of barbarous warfare.' It continued: '... the shock which would have been given to every section of the South African society by the sight of the uncivilised blacks and English soldiers, shoulder to shoulder in a war against a white race.'[3]

This was the main reason for the Boer attitude towards arming blacks, and it later strengthened even more during military operations. The war lasted for almost three years and Britain's need to use blacks in a supporting role increased. During the early stages of the war there were constant accusations from both sides regarding the breaking of the silent agreement. Later Britain encouraged the coloured people to assist against the Boers on a massive scale and so achieve an early victory. When the guerilla phase of the war began to escalate, the boundaries of agreement widened dramatically. Apart from the building of blockhouses and general guard support by unarmed blacks, British forces gained success by using black spies against the commandos. During the scorched-earth policy they were also used to herd cattle from the decimated farms and were rewarded with a share of the loot. They also took part in the burning down of farmhouses and the rounding up of women, children and the elderly for the concentration camps. The original order was to use unarmed non-whites to perform these functions, but they were later armed so that they could protect themselves.[4]

The Boers also made use of black spies but never armed them.[5] Both parties executed captured spies on the charges of treason. The first black spy to be executed in the Cape Colony met his fate before a British firing squad. Alfred Malapi was captured in Aliwal North during December 1900 while spying against the British. He had been an informer for the Boers although he worked for the British.

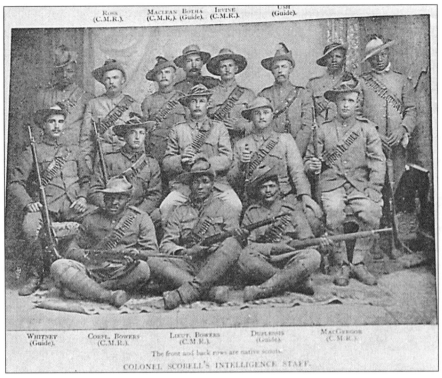

Colonel Scobell's hunting columns relied heavily on information received from black spies.
This is a photograph of the intelligence staff consisting of black and white colonists.
Source: After Pretoria, *by Wilson*

He was caught in British uniform and immediately shot.[6] The posting of non-white guards over the women and children in the concentration camps was tremendously offensive to the Boers. It was largely the evidence given by non-whites against captured Boers that brought the race question to breaking-point. This is evident in the number of executions carried out of black spies.[7] Many rebels were thrown into gaol on evidence extracted from non-whites who were rewarded with a few shillings.[8] The pain and suffering that resulted from Britain's scorched-earth policy and the internment of the population in concentration camps resulted in a proclamation being issued by the Boers. Generals De Wet and Kritzinger announced a policy of retaliation against loyalists in general. Houses could be burnt down, and non-whites caught for spying or being in uniform would be summarily executed.[9] This order was issued mainly to the commandos operating in the Cape Colony, where guerilla warfare raged. Later in the year another proclamation was issued regarding the capture of messengers in the employ of the British forces. If there was any suspicion that their activities were detrimental to the Boers they should be summarily executed.[10] The position now was very clear, and the Boers had received official notification that revenge could be taken for the hated scorched-earth policy proclaimed by Kitchener against the Republics.

Kitchener used this as an excuse to arm non-whites on a large scale.[11] It must be mentioned that he was forced to make this decision because of the shortage of troops in the escalating guerilla campaigns. By March 1902 there were 5435 non-whites under arms in the British forces in the Cape at that time. The total throughout the country was in the region of 30 000 non-whites under arms, which was greater than the entire Boer fighting forces.[12]

The deployment of such a large force across the vast regions of the Northern Cape formed the foundation of the eventual racial war that followed.[13] The past tradition of the Boers was one of non-participation by non-whites during a conflict period, but the arming of so many of them became a real military threat. Reprisals against non-whites involved with the British military now took on a new dimension, and were viewed by the Boers as being a deterrent, as well as a possible disruption of a Black-British alliance, and to discourage the British from taking that route.[14]

The floggings and executions of coloured spies, messengers and sympathisers now reached alarming proportions, and was cause for great concern. As a deterrent, Kitchener began executing burgers who were charged with the 'murder' of coloured troops under arms. These acts were now to be classified as war crimes, and not only rebels, but burgers of the Republics could be executed for them.[15] On 19 August 1901, in Graaff-Reinet, Petrus Fourie became the first burger to be executed for the murder of a non-white spy.

Only after the executions of several Boers, including Commandant Lötter, did Smuts and Kritzinger issue orders to stop the executions of non-whites, even if caught in uniform and armed.[16] In future they would be classed as ordinary soldiers by the Boers. However, the Cape rebel was never to enjoy that privilege.

CHAPTER 16

Attack on the Border Scouts Near Kenhardt

arly in 1901 the Boer commandos penetrated into the vast expanses of the Northern Karoo and Bushmanland. The British had to rely upon the coloured community for the defence of the region, and in May established the Border Scouts to patrol the districts of Upington and Kenhardt, consisting of about 800 coloured men commanded by British officers. The Namaqualand Border Scouts, consisting of 362 troops, and the Bushmanland Borderers, with 600 rank and file, were also set up.[1] Many of these men were outstanding shots, good horsemen and familiar with the areas under patrol.

The execution at De Aar of the Nienaber brothers and Nieuwoudt in March 1901, because of false evidence given by non-whites, was the spark that ignited racial warfare. The three burgers were condemned for the derailment of a train near a small station outside Hanover. This incident, as well as the murder of several wounded Boers by coloured soldiers, was the reason for swift retaliation by the commandos. Many harsh acts and executions were carried out by the Boers on captured coloured troops.[2]

Commandant Conroy then issued a proclamation advising that non-whites were not to be recognised as combatants in the struggle between Boer and Brit. He followed this up with a methodical campaign and was eventually held answerable for 71 deaths.[3] After peace was declared Conroy escaped to Europe to avoid prosecution for these killings, as Cape rebels were not granted amnesty.

He later returned in secrecy and assumed various disguises to hide his true identity. When he surfaced, he was tried for the allegation against him.[4]

In May 1901 Conroy took charge of the Kakamas rebels. He immediately set about to find coloured men under arms and spies who were relaying details of Boer positions to the British. On 23 May he recklessly attacked a patrol of Border Scouts with a small commando of 25 men at N'Roegas, a mere 12 miles from Kenhardt. He fell into a carefully planned ambush in pursuing a handful of Border Scouts. From well-entrenched positions on the surrounding hills, the Border Scouts, under the command of a British officer, met them with a withering fusillade. Conroy shot his way through with his revolver, killing two, and escaped with 12 of his men. Seven Boers were killed instantly, others badly wounded and two were captured.

When Conroy returned with reinforcements, the Scouts had disappeared. The wounded had been killed by having their skulls crushed. He continued carrying out his proclamation by executing captured coloured troops out of hand.[5]

The two captured burgers were escorted to Kenhardt and interned. Abraham Jooste had run out of ammunition and Hendrik Jacobs had been shot through the foot. The scene was now set for a warning to all Kenhardt rebels and for revenge on Conroy for his executions of coloured soldiers.

Abraham Christiaan Jooste (20)
Hendrik Lourens Jacobs (23)[6]
Executed by firing squad at Kenhardt on 24 July 1901.

Jooste, a young man from Boven Narries, and Jacobs, from the penal colony in Kakamas, were tried by Military Court in Kenhardt on 3 July 1901. The Court consisted of: *
Capt. JT White. Cape Police. District 2. O/C Troops, Kenhardt.
Lt. WM Eustace. Cmdt. Town Guard. Acting Chief Cmdt. Kenhardt.
Lt. ON McLeod. O/C Settle's Scouts.
Prosecutor: Lt. CH West. Cmdt. Town Guard, Kenhardt.
Defence: Mr Martin Sachs, Attorney, Kenhardt.
Evidence for the prosecution: Capt. JRB Rambottom of the Border Scouts. Sgt.-major WO Bowers of the Border Scouts. Mr HAG Hain and Mr J Pierce of Kakamas.

*Attorney-General's Report. AG 3560/3636. Blue Book Ref 21. Cape Archives
AG 3560/3636. Blue Book Ref 23. Cape Archives

CHARGES AGAINST JOOSTE

High treason and murder.

High treason for a second time. Still under oath from the first rebellion.

Being in arms against British forces.

Being in possession of expanding cartridges.

Previously found guilty of concealment of arms during September 1900.

(It appears that he spent time in gaol at Upington on this charge.)

CHARGES AGAINST JACOBS

High treason and murder.

High treason for a second time. Still under oath from the first rebellion.

Being in arms against British forces.

Being in possession of lead-tipped bullets.

Both were found guilty on all charges and sentenced to death by hanging. This sentence was ratified by Kitchener. On 23 July the town commandant notified the Kenhardt Dutch Reformed Church minister that the two men would be executed the following day and that he was free to visit them in the cells. Jooste was resigned to his fate but complained about the waiting period.

Jacobs still believed that a reprieve was possible. The two young men wrote farewell letters to their families from the prison. Jooste wrote:

Kenhardt, 23 July 1901

My dearest Father, Mother, Brothers and Sisters,

At last I take the pen to let you know that I and brother Hendrik Jacobs will depart tomorrow from this time into eternity. I depart with comfort because I know that the Lord is with me and will remain with me until my last breath. Then I will be with Him forever. So, my parents, brothers and sisters, be comforted in your thoughts because we will all meet again with God. This will be in heaven and that is a safe place. Before I depart I want to appeal to you all to stay with the Lord. Call on him while you still have the opportunity to do so. Bring all the children up in the fear of the Lord. Please see that Frans will follow the correct path. Ach! little Abraham was so precious to me and I love him very much. I have nothing more to write although I do feel like doing so.

I greet you, my Father, Mother, Brothers and Sisters with a last kiss. Farewell, my Parents, Brothers and Sisters, farewell! farewell! Here is a hymn in memory of me:

The Lord will arrive in the still of night

When all is calm and quiet
And blessed are those that wait for Him
With candles and lamps at trim
Build on the rocks and not on sand
When needed He will offer His hand
How bitter it could always seem
If fully prepared you have not been.
Yours,
Abraham Christiaan Jooste

During the evening prior to his execution, Jooste wrote a moving letter to his beloved, Frederika Booysen. The letter, in his own handwriting, was given to us by Frederika's grandson, Dr Fanie van der Walt of

Kenhardt,
28ᵗᵉ Julië, 1901.

Miss Fredrieka Booysen,

myn zeer beminde vriendin, heden neem ik voor het laatst de pen in my hand om u een paar letters te schryf, dat ik morgen vertrek met Broeder Hendrik Jacobs uit den tyd in den eeuwigheid. maar een troos heb ik; myn Verlosser leef, en ik zal ook leef, en onze God en Heer eere geef, en ik hoop u allen daar te ontmoet. Ik kan u niet veel schryf, maar ik hoop gy zal deze brief aan al myn vrienden geef. Zo wil ik u met allen groet met een kus der liefde, en al de andere. Ik hoop u allen daar boven te ontmoeten; in het byzonders zal ik u verwag totdat gy komen zal. maar hier op deze aarde wil ik u vaarwel zeggen en de andere ook. Geef aan Oom Frikkie ook de brief en aan Oom Willem ook. Zo groet ik u allen weder met een kus der liefde, en vaarwel, vaarwel, vaarwel myn beminde vriendin,

Abraham Christiaan Joosten.

Pretoria. His grandmother has kept this heirloom intact over the years.

Hendrik Jacobs also wrote a last letter from his death cell to his family, and Kobus Jooste of Upington kindly supplied us with a copy. The letters from a diary he has in his custody have been affected by time but we include some of the last writings.

On the morning of their execution they were permitted to hold a prayer meeting with their fellow prisoners. The message was: 'May the blessing of our Lord Jesus Christ, the Almighty Father and the Son and the Holy Spirit be with you now and forever more.' After the prayer meeting they all shook hands and bade farewell to the two condemned men.

The execution took place to the south of the town along the Brandvlei–Cape Town road under a large camelthorn tree. Because there were no gallows erected the men died before a firing squad. As was the custom they were tied to chairs, shot and buried immediately. After the burials oxen were driven over the area so as to eradicate all traces of their last resting places.

Death certificates issued for Jooste and Jacobs were identical.*

I certify that the sentence of death passed by the Court and confirmed by the General Chief in command was duly carried out at 4.30 pm on the 24th day of July 1901 at Kenhardt in the presence of the white troops of the guards and with male residents of the town.

As no means of hanging were available, the prisoner Abraham Christiaan Jooste was shot by a firing party of the 3rd Welsh Regiment.

JF White. Cape Police 11, Cmdt.
President of the Court
Kenhardt
24th July 1901

MEDICAL CERTIFICATE

I was present at the shooting of the accused Hendrik Lourens Jacobs on the 24th of July 1901 and certify that death was practically instant.

E Curtin   M.D.M.S.
Civil Surgeon, i/c troops.
Kenhardt
July 24th 1901

* Attorney-General's file.   AG 3560/3636. Blue Book refs: 21 & 23.
Class II Rebels 44/137 & 154/125

Letter from the Cape law department regarding the executed:

To: Regional Magistrate
Kenhardt

Subject: Trial of Jooste and Jacobs by Court Martial.
What has been the result of the trial of these men by Court Martial? Are these the same men who were placed on the list of Class II Rebels?

HR Dale
For Secretary, Law Department,
Cape Town

Reply: Jooste and Jacobs were sentenced to death and were executed on the 24th July last. These are the same men who were placed on the list of Class II rebels.

CA Pentz
Acting Res. Magt.
Kenhardt
Received by the Attorney-General's Office, Cape Town, 4/11/1901.

In December 1945 a monument was erected under the auspices of the Reddingsdaadbond to honour Jooste and Jacobs and those who died at N'Roegas. This memorial stands next to the road on the south side of Kenhardt where the old gaol was situated.

The memorial stone erected outside Kenhardt in memory of Abraham Jooste and Hendrik Jacobs.
Photograph: Graham Jooste

CHAPTER 17

The Siege
of Mafeking

In November 1901 five Boers were sentenced to death in Mafeking for the murder of non-whites during the siege the previous year. Two of them, Renike and Brink, were hanged in public at the gaol on 28 December after being found guilty by a Military Court. Due to mitigating circumstances, the other three were sentenced to life imprisonment, but not before all five had to carry the gallows from the station to the gaol.[1]

A large crowd had gathered at the gaol, including many blacks who displayed a great interest in the proceedings. To them this was tangible evidence of punishment for the death of blacks during the siege.[2]

These executions were a result of occurences during General JLP Snyman's blockade of the town during the siege, when he issued orders that any blacks caught plundering outside the perimeter of Mafeking should be shot out of hand. During the seven-month siege about 800 blacks were armed by the British to assist in the defence, but towards the end they were to suffer the most. Hundreds died from hunger and black gangs were formed, which crept out at night to raid surrounding farms in search of food.[3] Field-Cornet Arnoldus Renike and a group of burgers were ordered to raid and punish a certain location; which they did, and no prisoners were taken. In another incident, Louis Brink shot and killed a black looter who was armed with an assegaai.[4]

On 12 June 1901, more than a year after the relief of Mafeking, a number of Boers were captured, including the five who were sentenced to death.

Field-Cornet Arnoldus Renike[5]
Hanged at Mafeking on 28 December 1901.

Renike was an elderly man from Papesvlakte in the Mafeking district who joined a Transvaal commando as a Cape rebel. He maintained to the end that he was entirely innocent and did not deserve to be hanged for following orders from his superiors. He was quite resigned to his fate and stated that he had already suffered so much in this world that he had no desire to live any longer.

He was calm and strong while walking to his death with young Louis Brink, and reassured him with the words: 'Have courage, brother, we will speedily arrive in the splendour of heaven.'

There appears to have been a chance of clemency, but he seemed uninterested and met his death calmly and with dignity.

Louis Brink (21)
Hanged at Mafeking on 28 December 1901.

The 21-year-old Brink came from the farm Faith in the Mafeking district. He was found guilty of the murder of an armed black looter. He maintained, however, that he had shot the man on orders from his commanding officer. He could not accept the death penalty and was hopeful of clemency right until the end.

He was desperate when told he was to be hanged. He later became calm and told the clergyman who was counselling him that he had been mistaken about receiving clemency. With calmness, he accepted his salvation and put his trust in Jesus. He was hanged with the elderly Renike.

Mafeking was one of the few towns that had a gallows, and they met their end in the courtyard of the local gaol.

The graves of these two burgers are unknown and no photographs could be found. Investigation revealed no known headstones or monument erected to them.

CHAPTER 18

The Windmill Gallows
of Vryburg

In October 1901 four rebels met their death by hanging in Vryburg. These executions were the aftermath of rebel activity in the surrounding district by the forces of Commandant JA van Zyl. The commandos were engaged in numerous clashes with the Coloured Corps commanded by British officers, during which many coloured scouts and officers died as a result of the raiding tactics employed by the Boers. Rebels who fell into British hands were tried by the Military Court in Vryburg, and four were to pay the ultimate penalty. Johannes Jansen and Nasie Rautenbach were hanged on 11 October, followed by the Kuhn brothers on the 23rd.[1]

Because there were no gallows available in Vryburg, an ingenious plan was devised to hang them. The lower half of a windmill was used as the gallows. The platform and trapdoor were constructed of heavy timber beams, which were secured to the lower framework of the windmill. Removable rough wooden steps were made, and this unique gallows was erected near the main entrance of the gaol, the execution being carried out in public.

Lucas Fourie, a rebel who received clemency, told how the beams were later auctioned in public and that a farmer, Cornelius Halgryn, upon purchasing them, found bloodstains on the wood. It appears that troops bayoneted the hanging bodies to make sure they were dead. The bodies were loaded onto a zinc wagon and Fourie had to wash the bed of the cart.

The bodies were placed in shallow graves dug by Boer prisoners outside the southwest wall of the gaol. In 1929 the bodies were exhumed and reburied because of renovations to the prison walls. A monument was erected in their honour against the wall of the old gaol.[2]

Johannes Gert Wolfaardt Jansen (30)
Nicolaas Claassen Rautenbach (24)
Hanged at Vryburg on 11 October 1901.

Jansen and Rautenbach were members of the Vryburg rebel commando under Commandant Johannes van Zyl, which carried out guerilla warfare in the latter half of 1901 in Bechuanaland and Griqualand West. They were captured after a bloody encounter at Masiet in the Mafeking district on 3 September. British casualties were heavy, and during the running fight that ensued Jansen and Rautenbach were cut off from the commando.

Charged with being in possession of dumdum bullets, they testified that their commandant had ordered the commando to dispose of these bullets, which had been taken from the British on the previous day. Further charges brought against them were that Jansen had stolen four horses and Rautenbach 14 donkeys. They maintained that they did not use the dumdum bullets against the British and that the rounding up of horses and donkeys was an order they had to carry out. They were condemned to death by the Military Court. Two other burgers received clemency but were given long prison terms with hard labour.

Jansen was a married man with four children. His wife and children were sent to the Kimberley concentration camp during the same month that he joined the Boer forces. He was never to see them again.

Repeated requests to see his wife and children before his execution proved fruitless and he died on the gallows on 11 October with his friend Nasie Rautenbach.

Johannes Jansen of the farm New York, Vryburg.
Source: Hoe Zij Sterven

His wife read about his execution in a newspaper dropped in front of her tent by a British soldier. The couple's youngest child, Hendrik, was born in the camp six months after Jansen joined his commando. Their daughter, born shortly before the outbreak of war, died in the camp two weeks after her father was executed.

The prison warder told how Jansen spent the entire night before his execution on his knees in prayer and meditation. In the early hours of the morning he softly sang.

'Raise our hands to highest heaven,
Look upon the sanctuary on high ...'

From his cell, he wrote this letter to his wife:

Vryburg, 10 October 1901

To my beloved wife, CS Jansen.
Dearest,
I must inform you that with me it is going sadly. I have been condemned to death and will be hanged at 8 o'clock tomorrow morning. Thanks to God that I am not a murderer.

Dearest darling, you must be satisfied, because there is a God that will care for you and the orphans. Dearest, my heart feels so embittered that I cannot write properly. Darling, if you marry again please ask the Lord for a man who will take care of the children.

Furthermore, my dearest, when once there is peace again you must go to Dirk Groenewald who is keeping four oxen and a cow for us. Oelf Hennay has a further five oxen. At Onveiligspan you will find a horse and saddle as well as three oxen belonging to my brother Hendrik. I left them in the care of the Swart family.

I will now stop writing. It is tough going.

With heartfelt kisses to my wife and children whom I will never see again on this earth, but only in Heaven with Jesus.

Keep Jesus before you always,

My sorrowing soul awaits the death.
JGW Jansen

Nasie Rautenbach was a 24-year-old bachelor from Massaukop near Vryburg. This fiery young burger had previously served under General De la Rey in the Kimberley and Schweizer-Reneke regions and had participated in several pitched battles. He testified in his trial that everything he had done was on orders received from his commandant. The dumdum bullets found on him were, in fact, taken from British soldiers the day before he had been captured, but he had never used any.

The evening before his execution he asked a fellow prisoner whether it was a difficult death to be hanged. The bearded old man answered: 'No, death is immediate, the hardest is to climb onto the gallows.' Rautenbach replied: 'Well, if that is the case, then I am satisfied. I will now gladly give up my life for my country and its people.'

Nicolaas Rautenbach of Massaukop, Vryburg.

Later that evening he was visited by his mother who was only permitted to be with him for 20 minutes. The prison warder reported that Rautenbach fell into a peaceful sleep at about one o'clock with his arms folded across his chest. On the morning of his execution he was asked by the guard if he required anything and his request for a mug of coffee was granted. He was hanged at about 8 o'clock that morning with Johannes Jansen.

On the morning of 11 October, Jansen and Rautenbach climbed the rough wooden steps to the platform full of smiles. They gallantly bowed to the Boers and townspeople who had been summonsed to attend the executions. The previous evening Jansen had cut off his moustache with his penknife. The hair and a photo of him are preserved in the Vryburg museum. A memorial was erected at the old gaol in memory of the four who were hanged at Vryburg.

Field-Cornet Hermanus (Manie) Kuhn (43)
Johannes (Jurie) Kuhn (42)
Hanged at Vryburg on 29 October 1901.[4]

Two weeks after the public hangings of Jansen and Rautenbach the town of Vryburg again played witness to a hanging spectacle, this time that of the Kuhn brothers. The Kuhns were prosperous farmers from the farms Soetlief and Graspan to the north of Vryburg. Manie held the rank of field-cornet in the rebel commando of Commandant JA van Zyl, who operated in the regions of Vryburg and Mafeking. Before their capture the commando was involved in a skirmish of major proportions on the farm Mooifontein, west of Vryburg. During the fight an entire patrol of black scouts and their officers was almost annihilated.

Manie and Jurie paid a hurried visit to their farm Soetlief for provisions. They were still busy packing when a British patrol arrived and surrounded them. Manie managed to slip out of the back door but his horse was nowhere to be seen. He ran into the bushes and hid behind the kraal wall where he buried a small bag of money. The patrol rode him down and he was captured. His brother Jurie was taken inside the house.

Manie was accused of the murder of a black Scout at Mooifontein. He stated that as a result of the heavy firing it was impossible to say who was responsible for the death of various British troops. He was, however, found guilty and after a month's internment was hanged in public at Vryburg. His 15-year-old son was sentenced to six months imprisonment for aiding and abetting the Boers.

The brothers' identical death certificates stated as follows:

Manie Kuhn of Zoetlief, Vryburg.
Source: Hoe Zij Sterven

I hereby certify that the prisoner JJ Kuhn was executed by hanging at 8 am today.*

Death certificate herewith.

Vryburg
29/10/1901
WHE Murray Lt.-Col.
Cmdt.

* MEDICAL˙CERTIFICATE

I hereby confirm that the cause of death was:
(a) Primary hanging
(b) Asphyxia
(c) Fracture of spinal column.

WM Nugent
District Surgeon
29/10/1901
Vryburg

Before he was executed, Manie told his son where he had hidden the money. The youngster found the money before his mother and her four young children were interned in the concentration camp at Vryburg. This was all they had to restart their lives after the war. The farmhouses had been destroyed and looted after the skirmishes.

During the early morning of his execution, his family arrived from the Vryburg concentration camp on a wagon. They had been granted permission to say farewell to him. Heartrending scenes followed as his wife and children were torn from him when his time for the gallows arrived.

During his internment at the Vryburg gaol, he made a small Bible out of a piece of soapstone, as well as a small eating fork from his penknife. Both these articles are to be found at the museum in Vryburg, as well as a photograph of him.

Jurie acknowledged that he was in the farmhouse when the Boers fired on a British patrol and a black Scout was killed, but denied having

* Ref AG 3636/AG 3560. Blue Book 37 and 43. M19 & M737 Cape Archives, Cape Town.

fired the fatal shot. He was also found guilty on all charges and a month later met his death on the windmill gallows of Vryburg. Jurie was a married man with a family, but very little is known of this reserved individual. His family did not visit him while he was gaoled in Vryburg, but Reverend H Moolman visited him in his cell the night before his execution and found a very calm person. Jurie stated that he was prepared to die for his country and his nation. As he climbed onto the scaffold, he prayed silently with calmness and dignity.

No photo of Jurie exists but his name is honoured on the monument at the old gaol in Vryburg, together with that of his brother.

The memorial plaque on the prison wall at Vryburg in memory of the four burgers who were hanged behind the Vryburg prison.
Photograph: Graham Jooste

CHAPTER 19

An Ordinary Soldier and No Rebel

Commandant Gideon Jacobus Scheepers was not a rebel. He was born in the Transvaal and entered the Cape Colony with a small commando of Free Staters to disrupt the British war effort. His main objective was to damage the communications networks and this included train-wrecking and tearing up of railway lines. Furthermore, he was to act against the loyalists with the object of discouraging them from aiding the British. The arming of coloured and black troops by the British was of considerable importance to the Boers. They maintained that it was a white man's war, and the subject was very irksome to them. Because of this Scheepers received orders to act against armed coloured and black soldiers, so as to discourage the British from using them. However, the main objective of the incursion was to incite the pro-Boer population into open rebellion.[1]

His military actions in the Colony achieved success, and were as legitimate as those of Hertzog, Malan, De Wet, Kritzinger, Lötter

Gideon Scheepers of Grootlaagte, Middelburg, Transvaal.
Photograph: War Museum of the Boer Republics

149

and Smuts, who all invaded the Cape Colony with similar objectives in mind. The carrying out of his orders did, therefore, not make him a war criminal and he should have been treated as a prisoner of war according to the Hague Convention.

In the case of Lötter, Van Wyk and many other burgers, their claims to being Transvaal or Free State citizens were totally rejected by the Military Court and they were executed as rebels.

However, in the case of Scheepers, this was not possible. The fact that the Scheepers and Lötter commandos consisted of about 80 per cent rebels made them the two most sought-after leaders of guerilla campaigns. Scheepers was charged with war crimes and not for being a rebel.

The question arises, was Scheepers guilty of the charges laid against him? Did he act beyond the norms of 'civilised warfare' or not? The Military Court appeared to have already come to a specific conclusion.

Scheepers was charged on nine counts of murder of coloured spies and also for attempted murder, 15 counts of arson, two counts of destroying trains and railway lines, as well as five counts of scandalous conduct and barbaric deeds contrary to the norms of civilised warfare.[2] His defence was that he had acted as any loyal Transvaal or Free State commandant would have done by carrying out orders received from his superiors in the chain of command.

When the British commenced their scorched-earth policy in the Republics, the Free State high command warned Kitchener that, unless he stopped the burning down of Boer farmhouses and the wanton destruction of crops and livestock, orders would be issued to the Boer commandos operating in the Cape Colony to retaliate. This would mean the burning of houses belonging to loyalists or anyone giving aid to the British forces in the Cape Colony, exactly as was being done in the Free State by the British forces.

In March 1901 such an order was issued by President Steyn and General De Wet. Scheepers now merely carried out these orders.[3] He openly admitted that he had burnt down certain houses, but avoided pleading guilty as it was not considered a punishable offence.[4]

The hypocritical attitude of the prosecutors in terming these acts 'war crimes' was commented upon by the British newspaper, the *Morning Leader*, after Scheepers received the death sentence: 'It is laughable that this man could be shot for a transgression which the British were first to commit during the South African War.'[5] It was therefore an accepted method of conflict and did not violate any norms of civilised warfare!

It was equally ludicrous to consider the destruction of trains and railway lines punishable as a war crime. It was the fundamental objective of every Boer commander to disrupt the British communications systems and should never have been described as a war crime. If Scheepers was guilty of this offence and paid for it with his life then every Boer commander falling captive should have been shot.

The sentencing of Scheepers for this crime was disgraceful. Furthermore, the findings of the Military Court as regards his cruelty towards captured spies rested purely on the evidence supplied by coloured and black troops. In his defence, he testified that false evidence had been led against him by these parties and that they were entirely unreliable witnesses. He could not call witnesses for his defence as they were all still on commando.

The Military Court accepted the evidence of the witnesses as truthful, which would not have been the case in an impartial court. He was therefore found guilty on false evidence.[6]

The sentencing of Scheepers on the evidence of such witnesses was echoed by Ramsay MacDonald, who stated in Parliament: 'Scheepers has been shot upon a verdict of a court that did not understand the first elements of justice and had not the faintest idea when a statement was proved'.[7] Furthermore, if Scheepers could be given the death penalty of 'barbarous acts contrary to the acts of civilised warfare' one wonders what would have happened to Kitchener's commanders and Brabant's Horse if they had appeared in court on charges of cruelty committed against defenceless and innocent women and children. These acts were therefore not classified as war crimes.

On the charges of arson, disruption of trains, the tearing up of railway lines and so-called barbaric acts contrary to civilised warfare, Scheepers would not have been found guilty if judged by a competent and unbiased court.[8]

The significant question in the Scheepers trial centred around his execution of coloured spies. Was this murder, or was it legitimate? In the first place, it must be noted that members of the coloured or black communities were not looked upon as being combatants.[9] From the beginning of the conflict, the British were aware that the Boers considered the war to be a white man's war, and were against them being armed in any way. According to General Smuts, there was only one occasion when the Boers made use of armed blacks in an attack. This was during the siege of Mafeking when Commandant PA Cronje armed a few blacks to guard a Boer installation, without the authority of his superiors.[10] The British also considered the rebels to be non-combatants and thus felt vindicated when executing them. Similarly, the Boers adopted this attitude when executing black spies whom they did not consider to be part of the British forces.

The perception grew when it became clear that the British were arming blacks on a massive scale during the guerilla-warfare period. This turn of events obliged General Kritzinger to issue a proclamation during July 1901, wherein he ordered that all blacks captured in the service of the British, whether armed or not, should be summarily executed. During November a further proclamation was issued, ordering that any black or coloured persons betraying the whereabouts of Boer commandos to the British should be executed when caught.

There was therefore to be no difference between a 'Scout' and a 'spy'.[11] The British reacted to this proclamation by executing all Boers found guilty of 'murdering' coloured people or blacks.

Scheepers did not dispute the fact that he had executed certain coloured spies, but denied other instances. He drew the court's attention to the dubious evidence laid against him by the witnesses and to the fact that he was denied the right to call his own witnesses. He also brought to notice the unfairness of the proceedings whereby all evidence heard against him was accepted as the truth, but his own testimony had been rejected, asking how he could be tried before such a prejudiced court.[12]

The fact that Scheepers admitted to the execution of some spies did not make him guilty of murder. The conclusion that 'he was rightly convicted' when there was evidence that he had executed an informant was therefore wrong.[13] He would only have been found guilty if he had committed a war crime by acting in an unlawful manner, that he had acted without orders from higher authority, or that his actions were contrary to civilised warfare. This was certainly not the case as the rules had been made by the British military hierarchy.

The question could well be asked if the Military Court had any jurisdiction over this hearing at all. Scheepers was a Transvaler serving with a Free State commando and received his orders from President Steyn and General De Wet. That his trial in the Cape Colony by a Military Court and the subsequent findings prompted various British officers to comment that 'he was not treated in the manner befitting a soldier' spoke volumes.[14]

With regard to Scheepers acting upon orders received from higher authority, it is fitting to compare the verdict given by a better-equipped court in another area.

In June 1900 a British trooper named Smith was tried by a Military Court in Colesberg for the murder of a black. His superior officer, Captain Fox, had ordered him to 'blow a hole through this black', which he promptly did. The reason for this immediate execution was that the black had disobeyed orders and that he could not produce a missing set of reins. The finding of the court was that Smith had not acted unlawfully by obeying his orders.

He would only have been found guilty if it was 'evident' that he would be committing an unlawful act, and then he would have been compelled to disobey the order. Given the war situation, Fox's orders were not entirely irregular and would have been carried out by any reasonable person. Therefore trooper Smith had not acted unlawfully in carrying out this order from his commanding officer. He was found not guilty and returned to the ranks. Did Scheepers have any reason to disobey his orders because it was 'evident' that they were unlawful?[15]

During the peace negotiations at Vereeniging, Commandant Barend Cilliers of the Kroonstad commando was denied amnesty and charged with the murder of Lieutenant Boyle, a British officer. The allegation against Boyle by the Boers was that he had ravaged Boer women and children and burned farmhouses as part of the scorched-earth policy ordered by Kitchener. Cilliers was ordered by General Philip Botha to execute Boyle, which was duly done. Unluckily for Cilliers his superior officer was killed in action at Doornberg near Ventersburg shortly afterwards. During his trial he called on General De Wet as a witness.

De Wet asked the prosecuting officer if he expected obedience from his men at all times. He received the emphatic answer 'yes'. The case against Cilliers was dismissed as the court found that he had acted upon orders from his superiors and it was evident that he had not acted unlawfully.[16]

Verdicts like this left no doubt of the prejudice of the Military Courts. In his thesis on the Military Courts, Dr Snyman came to the conclusion that verdicts were justified because 'these Courts did not bother much about the law and justice. They were there to please the immediate higher authorities', and furthermore that 'it was very apparent that no defence on earth would have made an impression on these courts'.[17]

The trial of a celebrated Boer commandant of the calibre of Scheepers charged with war crimes was a very problematic and thorny issue for the British. This was highlighted by secret coded telegrams received by the Military Court president from the highest authority of the occupying forces. He was instructed to proceed with haste and urgency; testimony that reasonable justice had nothing to do with the matter.[18]

A note of despair rings in the words of Scheepers who commented after his trial and conviction: 'This whole business looks as if it is a farce from beginning to end. How can I and other condemned innocent persons be accused of unlawfulness before a court like this? Is it possible for me to appear before such a court?'

The court consisted of the following:

President	Lt.-Col. P Sprot	The Carbineers
	Capt. CE Wilson	Lancashire Fusileers
	Lt. TP Dawson	PAGMI
Prosecutor	Mr EC Tennant	
Defence	Mr T Auret	

With his execution, Gideon Scheepers passed into the realm of everlasting folklore and martyrdom as one who died for his country and its people. This symbol of ordinary soldiers who were executed as criminals rings from the poem by DJ Opperman:

'He was an ordinary warrior, Lord, and no rebel.'

Commandant Gideon Jacobus Scheepers (23)[19]
Executed by firing squad at Graaff-Reinet on 18 January 1902.

Scheepers was of gentle character and very religious. His ambition was to become a minister of religion but this was not possible because of a lack of funds. He joined the Transvaal Artillery instead as this would give him a monthly income. At the young age of 22, he had been promoted to officer commanding the newly formed Free State heliograph section. At the outbreak of hostilities with Britain, he was seconded to the commando of General CR de Wet. Under De Wet's leadership, he became proficient as a scout and was soon earmarked for higher command.

With the commencement of guerilla activities, this mature young soldier was promoted to commandant of a small commando of hand-picked men. He was ordered into the Cape Colony to prepare the way for a full-scale invasion envisaged by generals De Wet and De la Rey.

Gideon Scheepers with the heliograph division of the Free State Artillery.
Source: Rondom die Anglo-Boereoorlog, *by Kriel and De Villiers*

Scheepers became famous among the Boers for his reprisals against the scorched-earth policy of Kitchener. Notorious among the British military and the loyalists of the Cape Midlands, he was eagerly hunted by them. He gained early successes and was known for his daring and legendary escapes.

On 30 July 1901, his commando was dealt a severe blow by the outstanding British commander Colonel Harry Scobell. A fast-moving column that included many colonials cornered him at Onbedacht in the Graaff-Reinet district and captured 30 of his men. He managed to escape with the remainder of his commando and continued to harass the British in the Cape Midlands and further south as well.

During this period, Scheepers burnt numerous loyalist homes and executed a number of coloured spies. He was however unsuccessful in breaking the strong bond that existed between the native population and the occupying British forces.[20] Already the tide was turning against him and he became very ill.

There has always been controversy about the cause of his sudden decline in health. Among the possible reasons were acute appendicitis, severe stomach ailments, fever and, according to Shearing, a possibility of maniacal depression.[22] It appears that one Hugo joined the Scheepers commando as a cook a few days before he and his adjutant were poisoned, and then disappeared overnight. (Hugo was the brother of Judge HJ Hugo and a spy in the service of the British.)

On 9 October his commando was obliged to leave him behind on the farm Koppieskraal in the Prince Albert district, notifying the military authorities of his condition and that he required immediate medical attention.

Scheepers was treated in Beaufort West while under strict military guard and his health improved slowly. His nemesis, Colonel Scobell, visited him on numerous occasions and the hours sped by as they discussed their many skirmishes. Scobell held Scheepers in high esteem and was always friendly towards him. Scobell wrote in his diary: 'He is evidently a very clever fellow. He told me I was called the Night Devil by his men.'[23]

On 14 November 1901 Scheepers, although very ill, was entrained for Graaff-Reinet. During the trip, he became so ill that he had to be treated at the hospital in Noupoort. After his partial recovery he was

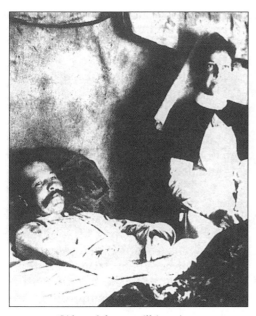

Gideon Scheepers ill in prison.
Photograph: War Museum
of the Boer Republics

transported to Graaff-Reinet to stand trial. The trial commenced on 18 December, but had to be postponed on numerous occasions because Scheepers was too weak to attend. The prosecution called 53 witnesses, among them Jan Momberg, a former member of the Scheepers commando who had also testified against Jan van Rensburg in exchange for clemency from his death sentence. The defence could only muster three witnesses, as the rest were still on active services.[24]

On 28 December, the Military Court reached its verdict: guilty on 29 charges out of 30. On 17 January the sentence was proclaimed before the population of Graaff-Reinet on the church square. A shaking Colonel Henniker announced that Scheepers was to die before a firing squad. As the band started playing *God Save the Queen* a soldier plucked Scheepers' hat off and threw it to the ground. Scheepers pushed the soldier in the chest and replaced the hat firmly on his head. He then calmly turned around and made his way back to the ambulance wagon. He was advised in his cell that he would be executed the next day.

At 3 pm the following day, Scheepers was placed in an ambulance wagon and driven down the main street to the place of execution about two kilometres from town on the Murraysburg road. Only Reverend AC Murray was allowed to accompany him. A request by Scheepers that he should not be shot by colonials was granted and the firing squad was made up of Coldstream Guards. His requests not to be blindfolded or tied were refused by the officer in charge. He could however be buried with his favourite white-banded hat and ostrich feather. The photographer IH Allan of Graaff-Reinet, who was ordered to photograph the execution, stated that Scheepers walked towards his

Scheepers leaving the hotel at the Cango Caves on the last stage to Prince Albert.
He can be seen in front of the window wearing a black feather in his hat.
He was already seriously ill.
Source: Rondom die Anglo-Boereoorlog, *by Kriel and De Villiers*

grave fearlessly and calmly. He stopped and peered into the open grave and a mocking smile appeared around his lips before he sat down on the chair. Wilfred Harrison, a member of the firing squad, stated that death must have been instantaneous. The body was untied, the chair broken up and thrown into the grave with his hat. The band played the popular army tune *More Work for the Undertaker.* He was placed on a blanket and the command given: 'Let him drop'. Unslaked lime was poured over the body and the grave filled in. It was later reported that during the night a fight broke out among troops in the barracks as a result of the execution.

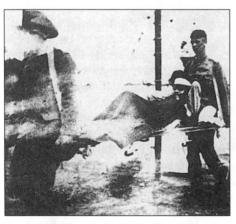

Scheepers on his way to his trial.
Source: War Museum of the Boer Republics

Lieutenant Dawson later stated that a fearful Colonel Henniker had the body dug up during a thunderstorm that night and reburied elsewhere. To this day, the remains of Gideon Scheepers have never been found.

Scheepers is sentenced on the church square in Graaff-Reinet.
Source: War Museum of the Boer Republics

A small stone monument was erected to Scheepers on a rock-strewn hill about 100 paces from the place of execution, below the high-water mark of the present dam. According to the diary of the town commandant, Major Shute, the body was reburied lower down in the loop of the river.[25]

A monument of white marble was erected in Graaff-Reinet in the corner of a private property. Legend has it that a pro-British town council refused to sanction the erection of such a memorial on municipal property. It embodies General De Wet keeping guard over a fallen Scheepers with his Mauser. Scheepers' name appears on this monument along with the names of all those executed in Graaff-Reinet. In poems and prose, nobody is more revered than Gideon Scheepers, the exceptional martyr of the Anglo-Boer War.

Extracts from his diary give us not only an insight into the person of Gideon Scheepers, but also his deep concern about the diabolic treatment and executions of burgers accused as war criminals. About his surrender he writes:

These dramatic photographs of Scheepers' execution were secretly taken by a British soldier. It later fell into the hands of MJ Leibbrandt and is the only indication of the location of Scheepers' grave. In the top photograph, he is being tied to his chair, and in the bottom photograph, he is reeling back after the firing squad had hit their mark.
Photographs: Cape Archives

'At four o'clock the burgers were ready to ride, and a cart was inspanned for me. I tried my utmost to climb off the bed, but to no avail. I was thus compelled to surrender. I called my officers into the bedroom for a meeting regarding the position we found ourselves in. They were all for moving me by force, but I convinced them that my pain would be unbearable and a burden. I was also suffering from fever. So we had to say farewell. Each burger came in and bade me farewell with sadness. Some sat on and around

The memorial stone outside Graaff-Reinet on the road to Murraysburg, approximately 100 metres from the place where Gideon Scheepers was executed. The text reads:
'He lives in this country,
Now, and for evermore.'
Photograph: Graham Jooste

my bed and appeared to be agitated. My adjutant, the 16-year-old Karl Lehmkuhlt, brave and daring, placed his head against my chest and sobbed softly as the tears streamed down his cheeks. I never want to experience another day like that. [Witnesses later testified that Lehmkuhlt had also been poisoned.] My one consolation was that I had served my Government faithfully up until the last moment and did everything in my power to support our legitimate cause in a lawful and just manner.'

About his Afrikaner heritage he wrote: 'I am prepared to endure my punishment for my nation and country and President. Oh! and all those brave and noble men who have already died for our cause. How glorious it is to be crucified for our nation and especially for our religion. The enemy may delight in it, but the Afrikaner People will never die!

'I hope that my death will be the cause for great happenings in the future, that all commandants and officers who are still fighting will avenge me. If anyone of them happens to share the same fate as me, they must remember that it was for our nation and country ...'

'I always knew that the Englishman was a false character and has shed the blood of many innocents, but I never knew that they were so

161

dreadfully blind and could not see the truth. The Lord our God will judge.'

After he had received the death penalty, he wrote: 'And so it is today, the 17th of January 1902, that will be my last day on earth. It is terrible to think about it and a person wishes that the hour had already arrived. Oh! Lord, for how long will you allow this evil to continue?

'Save Your people, my God, and let justice happen!

'It is of great comfort to me that I have served my Government faithfully. If I had only known that I would have killed innocently, then I would have caused more damage to the enemy than I have done. All the allegations against me can be answered in one sentence, namely that I carried out my orders.

'Reverend Murray arrived to pray with me, but I refused, because his sympathy was for the enemy and I told him that it was not correct for me to pray with him. Later my attitude changed towards him and we prayed together for myself and my family. About ten o'clock that evening an officer came to me and advised me that I would not be executed at dawn, but sometime later during the day. At first I felt relieved, but later I longed it would be all over, the sooner the better.

'I slept from eleven to three and then started writing various letters, which are lying next to me. These are the letters to family and friends. I

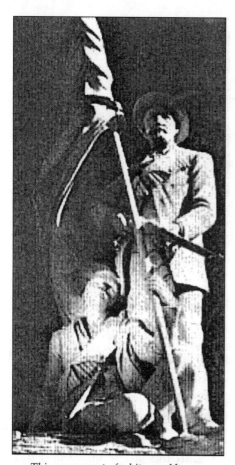

This monument of white marble was erected at Graaff-Reinet and is a symbolic depiction of the dying Scheepers with General De Wet keeping watch over him and carrying a Mauser.
Photograph: Rondom die Anglo-Boereoorlog, *by Kriel and De Villiers*

am now patiently awaiting my last hour. At midday the officer appeared again and told me that I was to be executed at five o'clock. So I am now writing my last letters and filling in my diary. It is with my best wishes and blessings to my friends and family and I trust and hope that we will meet someday at a better place ...'

He wrote no more, and was executed at about 3 pm.

After the war his mother tried desperately to get his last letters and his diary but her attempts proved fruitless. In an open letter to a newspaper she appealed to all the generals of the former Republics to help her to secure her son's papers, which had been carried away by Tennant, the public prosecutor. She wrote:

'We would dearly like to have the letters, as they were meant for us. They belong to us. The war is over. Why may they not be sent to us? Whatever we have tried through appeals and writings, everything has been in vain.'

Even more shameful was the refusal of the military authorities to assist in the return of the body of her son, who had always wanted to be buried on the family farm, Roodepoort, in the Middelburg, Transvaal district, on which he had been born. His mother wrote:

'In January after the war his father travelled to Graaff-Reinet to find his grave. He was notified that he had to receive special permission from Lord Milner to open the grave. In a friendly manner he requested His Lordship to open the grave of his son and to place a sheet of zinc over the body to preserve it from further damage. At a later stage, when convenient to His Excellency, and when he found the time appropriate, he could exhume the body and convey it to the Transvaal. No matter how my husband begged and pleaded with His Excellency, everything was refused. He was forbidden to open the grave and nobody wanted to show him the place of burial. Nobody could say: "Here your son lies buried."

'I am asking everybody with a honest heart, what mother can endure this? Which mother could forget her child who was so precious to her? Who could not kneel in sorrow when you thought of the last letter your son had written to you, and this is now cruelly being withheld from her. Who would not be overcome by despair and desperation because you could not fulfil the last wishes of your son to be buried at his birthplace? Is there any greater soul-destroying act that can be conceived by the cleverest and cruelest of persons to deny a mother to know where the grave of her son is?'

She continues her plea for someone to come forward to help her to establish if the rumour is true that he was still alive, or to send her details of his last resting place. She then ends her letter with an appeal to the editor of the newspaper:

The Editor

Dear Sir,
If you please, could anybody with information please contact your newspaper or write to me at the attached address.

Sophia C Scheepers
Roodepoort
Middelburg, Transvaal.

In the end, it was all for nothing. Her quest had failed. Her son's grave has never been found. Even in her nineties, Sophia Scheepers was tortured by uncertainty:

Was everything in vain?

Not really, because on his memorial it says: 'He lives in this land, now and for evermore!'[26]

CHAPTER 20

The Forgotten One

On 7 March 1902, nearly two months after the execution of Gideon Scheepers, the second in command of the British forces fell into Boer hands. Lord Methuen was Kitchener's right-hand man in the carrying out of his scorched-earth policy and the herding of women and children into concentration camps. He was wounded and captured during a Boer raid on his column at Tweebosch. The most hated of the British commanders, after Kitchener, was now a prisoner of war.[1]

The man who captured him was an outlaw Boer general whose home and farm had been devastated and his family forced to wander the veld avoiding British columns. This was General Koos de la Rey, commander of the Boer guerilla forces in the Western Transvaal. The commando strongly recommended that Methuen should be tried by a Military Court for the horrible deeds he had committed, but in one of the greatest conciliatory acts imaginable, De la Rey set Methuen free. He was loaded onto an ambulance wagon with all his possessions and taken to the nearest town for medical treatment. Mrs De la Rey, who had by now found her husband's commando, cooked him a chicken and baked him some rusks for the journey. Was De la Rey ignorant of the fact that the sick Scheepers had already been tried and dealt with in Graaff-Reinet?

The British newspaper, the *Morning Leader*, had this to say about the affair: 'This sort of chivalrous action surpasses our own conduct, by shooting Scheepers and Lötter, with scorn and in the strongest terms possible'.[2] But a month after the magnanimous release of Methuen, the

Boers were rewarded for their chivalry by the execution of a young rebel from the Eastern Cape Colony. One of the charges against him was the usual 'active in arms and attempted murder'. Would Kitchener have been aware of the gift of chicken and rusks that Mrs De la Rey gave to Methuen? We leave the question to the *Morning Leader*.

Francois Engelbertus du Randt (20)[3]
Executed by firing squad at Cradock on 5 April 1902.

Du Randt had been captured during a skirmish on 16 December 1901 at Koningskrans in the Cradock district, but was only brought to trial three months later, on 7 March, the same day that Methuen was released!

The chief witness for the prosecution was Jacobus van Heerden of the Cape Police, who was stationed at Cradock. Van Heerden testified that he had followed the tracks of horses and, in the ensuing skirmish, two rebels had been shot. The third had fired on him after raising a white flag. The accused had fired at them with a Martini-Henry rifle. (This rifle was a single-shot loader and its smoke could betray the position of the user.)

On this evidence, Du Randt was accused of attempting to 'murder' a British subject, while two of his companions lay dead next to him. Florence May Long from the Fort Beaufort district was called to the stand to testify that on 24 June a Boer commando had arrived at their farm store and commenced to plunder it and that Du Randt, who was known to them, was with the commando. On her testimony, Du Randt was charged with 'marauding' and theft.

Because he was armed and on commando, he was charged with high treason. Enough evidence was led to convict him on

Francois du Randt of Praambosch, Cradock.
Source: Hoe Zij Sterven

166

the charges laid against him. Sentence was proclaimed on the Cradock church square on 4 April 1902, and he died before the firing squad somewhere along the banks of the Fish River outside Cradock. His name appears on the monument in the church garden, but his grave is unknown.

Two months later, on 1 June, peace settled over the land and the firing squads were silent. Fransie du Randt was to be the last to die in this way in the Cape Colony.

The manner in which this fearless and courageous 20-year-old faced his death touches the heart. Reverend AC Murray witnessed this, the last execution of a Cape rebel. The following passage is a translation from *Hoe Zij Stierven*.

'Early in the morning of 4 April 1902 two rebels, Du Randt and Jan van Heerden, appeared on the market square in Cradock to hear the promulgation of sentence. They were surrounded by the Town Guard consisting of both white and black troops, and some mounted soldiers. In front of them stood the commandant and two officers. To the left was the magistrate, the mayor and some English clergy and a few other people. The interpreter stood between the commandant and the prisoners.

'Du Randt, a young man of about 25 [actually he had just turned 20] and with a charming face, strong-bodied and with broad shoulders, was ordered to step forward. He stood calm and upright as the death sentence was read in English and later interpreted into Dutch. Neither his bearing nor his appearance betrayed fear or dejection. He was charged on three counts: attempted murder, marauding and joining the enemy forces. He was found guilty on all charges and condemned to death by hanging. The sentence had been ratified by Lord Kitchener. Du Randt was then ordered to step back and Van Heerden had to step forward and take his place. The charges against Van Heerden were murder, attempted murder, joining the enemy forces, marauding and the destruction of a train. He was found guilty on all charges and condemned to death. However, his sentence was to be reduced to one of life imprisonment with hard labour and banishment.

'Du Randt openly discussed the matters of the day with everyone he came into contact with. He also advised what should be done with his belongings and settled down to write letters to his parents and family. At nine o'clock he had a quick bath and then a peaceful sleep for about four to five hours as one who had no conflict of conscience or soulsearching. When I asked the warder how he had behaved during the last moments of his life he informed me that Du Randt had not shown the least amount of fear. The military authorities decided that this execution should be strictly private and the place and time were kept secret. I was, however, told by a friend of mine who was an official in town.

'I awoke early on the morning of 5 April to find it was still dark outside. I arose immediately because the tragic scene, which I was about to witness, was clearly on my mind. The timepiece of a fellow human being had nearly run out. The words still spun around in my head: "To be shot! shot! at daybreak."

'And while these perilous words still rebounded in my mind I could see the coming image, which I would witness, very clearly. A strong young man, in the prime of health, would soon be a corpse.

'I dressed quickly in the candlelight and at quarter past five I heard some soldiers calling me. We went to the gaol on horseback. It was still dark and the moon gave off a weak reflection. We were the first to arrive at the gaol and found the night guard swinging his lantern from side to side. Shortly afterwards, Mr JJ van Rensburg arrived with a pass granting him permission to see the prisoner. I followed them to the cell of Du Randt and we found him standing at the door already dressed and with no sign of anxiety or alarm on his features or in his eyes. He had the appearance of a totally happy person.

'"Du Randt, my friend, do you know what is presently going to happen to you?" asked Van Rensburg.

'"Yes, I am totally prepared", was his calm answer.

'"Are you truthfully prepared to meet your God?" asked Van Rensburg.

"Yes, Uncle, fully prepared.'"

'I then stepped nearer and Van Rensburg introduced me to him. He answered that he knew me and had seen me often during my visits to the prisoners. He then stepped forward and offered me his hand and smiled: "Good morning, Doctor.[4] Have you come to say goodbye?"

'With a sorrowful voice and a lump in my throat I answered that I would see him again before the end. I then left them. When I passed through the outside door I came across the corporal of the guard.

Although he was very nervous and depressed he stressed his wonderment at the bravery of the young man who was to die so soon.

' "Good Heavens, what amazing spiritual strength this man has got!" cried the Corporal.

'In the street I came across the people who would be taking him to the grave. They had a four-seater Cape cart to which two strong mules were inspanned. An escort of 10 armed men took up positions in front and at the back of the vehicle. It was only slightly light now. The twilight of the grey morning gave the houses and nearby trees a sombre appearance as if nature itself was mourning with us. The sergeant of the detail shouted to the guards that everything was ready and that they should bring the prisoner out.

'As Du Randt was led out, he passed by the prison warder and with a smile said: "Good day, old man, a hearty thanks for all your friendliness." He was handcuffed to a soldier and accompanied by Van Rensburg. All three climbed onto the cart. Du Randt and the soldier were behind and Van Rensburg and the driver on the front seat. We rode slowly down the street. Everything was still and sad. Halfway through the town the commandant and an officer joined us. About a mile out of town my companion turned to me and remarked: "What a distance! What a gruesome task and how I hate it!"

' "Yes, it is gruesome work", I answered. "And just imagine how that poor man who is sitting there must feel, knowing that he will soon be a corpse within a quarter of an hour. Do you think you could meet death as calmly as he is doing?"

' "No, I do not think so", was his short answer.

'Exactly at 6 am we arrived at a grass-covered bank on the left-hand side of the Fish River, about a mile and a half from town. As yet the sun was not up, but there was sufficient light over 10 paces to be able to aim properly at an exposed place on a white shirt. Twelve soldiers under the command of a lieutenant and a sergeant stood in readiness. Ten paces behind stood a chair secured to two iron poles. Two paces behind the chair was the open grave. Du Randt was still tied to the soldier. He climbed down from the cart and walked bravely towards the chair. He sat down immediately. His right hand was untied. Van Rensburg and I followed him and stood before him.

' "Farewell, Brother", said Van Rensburg, "We will meet again in heaven."

' "Yes, Uncle, and sincere thanks for your interest in me", he answered. I then gripped his hand as a last farewell. He took my hand and greeted me cordially with "Good day". Even with the open grave behind him, he still smiled as he said farewell. Yes, truly, it was the smile of sweet innocence. For me it was an example of complete assurance of his everlasting salvation and happiness.

'The officer opened Du Randt's shirt and exposed his white vest which was to become the target. I placed my hand on his heart, but it was not even beating any faster. When Du Randt realised that they intended to tie his arms to the chair he looked up at Van Rensburg and said: "If they do not mind, I would prefer to be untied. I will sit very still." I translated his request to the soldier who answered in a friendly manner that he was compelled to carry out his orders. When I explained to Du Randt what had been said, he answered: "Do what must be done, I am fully prepared."

'Those were his last words. He only had to move an arm and a leg when they ordered him to be tied to the chair. There was no alarm to be seen on his face. Even his colouring remained the same. The handcuffs had to be removed and the blindfold placed around his eyes. The handcuffs gave a lot of trouble but eventually they were loosened. At last the soldier

An artist's impression of how Du Randt was executed.

stepped back and gave a sign to the lieutenant that everything was ready.

'Du Randt was now on his own. No friends, no family, no loving hand to caress him in the hour of his death. No mother or father to give him a farewell kiss and words of comfort and encouragement. There he sat with head held high and ready to die.

'The shrill orders of the lieutenant split the morning air:

' "Right about face!"

' "Present arms!"

' "Fire!"

'The Lee Metfords cracked.

'Du Randt gave a deep strangled sigh. His head fell forward and his arms shivered. He uttered one more weak sigh as his head rolled over backwards. I thought that he was dead, but he was still breathing. On his chest I saw small round, blue holes, three together in a line across his left chest. A shudder went through his body. A last sigh as the body slumped to be supported by the bonds that held him.

'He was dead and his soul had escaped to his everlasting home. His body was wrapped in a blanket and buried.'

And so the last Cape rebel died.

In the Attorney-General's files in the Cape Archives, under Section AG 3560 and AG 3636, the clinical blue pages of the charge sheet and accumulated reports tell us the following:

FRANCOIS ENGELBERTUS DU RANDT

From the Adelaide district. Born at Mankazana, Ft. Beaufort on 9/12/1881.
From Praambosch in the Cradock district. Captured at Honing Krantz (sic) Cradock district on 16/12/1901.
Date of trial. 7/3/1902 at Cradock.
Van Reenen's Commando.
Age 25 (sic)
Executed at Cradock 5/4/1902 by firing squad on banks of the Fish River.

MILITARY COURT
Lt. Col. GFH St John   Royal Artillery
Capt. H Chandos Pole Gell   Coldstream Guards
Lt. TP Dawson   PAGMI

CHARGES
Being actively in arms.
Marauding.
Attempted murder.

FOR THE PROSECUTION
Willem de Lange, his brother in law, testified that he had joined Van Reenen's commando.

James Long, had known him to be a British subject and the son of Jacob du Randt, from Praambosch, district Cradock.

Florence May Long, testified that he was present with the commando when they plundered their farm store at Konap Drift, Ft Beaufort district.

Jacobus van Heerden, who joined the Cape Police and followed the tracks which led to the skirmish.

Sworn before Lancelot Harrison, Dept. of Administration at Cradock. A statement was also given by C Milton, a special policeman who was with Jacobus van Heerden.

The separate charge sheet reads as follows:

CHARGE SHEET
The prisoner, Francois Engelbertus Durant (sic), a British subject of Praambosch, Fort Beaufort (sic) district now under Martial Law is charged with:
FIRST CHARGE
Being actively involved against Her Majesty's forces in that he at Praambosch, Ft Beaufort district on or about the 24th of June 1901, joined the armed forces of the enemy and served with them until captured at Honing Krantz in the Cradock district on the 16th of December 1901.
SECOND CHARGE
Marauding at Konap Drift.
In that he at Konap Drift in the Ft Beaufort district on or about 24th of June 1901 stole goods and property from one James Long, a British subject.
THIRD CHARGE
Attempted murder.
In that he at Honing Krantz on the 16th of December fired at certain British soldiers with intent to kill and murder them.
To be tried by Military Court by order of General French.
H Wilson   Capt
Cmdt. Cradock

Prisoner of war was born at Mankazana, Ft. Beaufort on the 9th of December 1881.
GFH St John   Lt. Col.   President Military Court

SENTENCE
Guilty on all charges and to be hanged.
REPORT BY MEDICAL OFFICER
This is to certify that Francois Engelbertus du Randt, a rebel, was shot this morning at 6 o'clock and death was instant.
Percy Beatty
M/O I/C Troops
Cradock
5/4/02

Co-author's note: The spelling of the drift was very irregular, ie. Konap Drift, Koonapdrift and Koonatsdrift.

Also, the district in which the farm Praambosch was situated, i.e.: Fort Beaufort, Cradock.

Also, the location of Du Randt's capture, i.e.: Koningkrans, Honing Krantz.

FRANSIE DU RANDT

In the cold grey of the morning,
Before the sun was dawning,
A knock on his door foretold,
That he should be ever so bold.

This was the moment of reckoning,
And his Lord was beckoning.
He was awake and ready,
With personality steady.

He was to meet his fate,
With accolades great,
He was truly a son,
When the war begun.

With patriotic flair,
And never to scare,
He threw in his lot.
But never to plot.

He was a boy from the Cape,
And could not escape,
The charges against him,
Were up to the brim.

What was the cause of this moment,
And the bailiff in torment,
He was condemned for marauding,
With supporters applauding.

He climbed on the cart,
With a cheerful heart,
The armed guard was there,
But never to scare.

The clip of the horses,
Strengthened his resources,
Only a mile to the grave,
And he would be brave.

The town was so silent,
And he was reliant,
On the strength of knowing,
God's blessings were flowing.

The dull Autumn moon,
Cast its shadows of doom,
Through the trees on the street,
With the horses clipped beat.

On the banks of Fish river,
The diggers did shiver,
The grave was complete,
The condemned one to greet.

With countenance still bright,
He did alight,

Handcutted to a soldier,
Walked shoulder to shoulder.

A chair had been placed,
Ten steps were paced,
The firing squad was ready,
Tried hard to be steady.

On the chair he sat down,
Without even a frown,
They unbuttoned his vest,
Exposed white on his breast.

Bound with ropes to the chair,
The soldiers did stare,
They seemed all to care,
For this boy would not scare.

He requested no blindfold,
But was quietly told,
By officer staid,
That orders were made.

He was left all alone,
A moment to atone,
The silence was broken,
By the order loudly spoken.

As the rifles spat death,
To stop his last breath,
He gave a strangled sigh,
And so was to die.

His grave was never found,
In Cradock's sandy ground,
But somewhere along the river,
Somebody will shiver.

As they read his sad tale,
Balanced on the justice scale,
It will be found to be wrong,
By an Earthly throng.

Graham Jooste

SECTION 2

Executions in
the Republics

The book *Hoe Zij Stierven* remains the most important source of information regarding the executions that took place in the Cape Colony during the Anglo-Boer War. Many of the old guard still say today that this was the first book about the war they read when they were young, and that the moving farewell letters of the condemned still move them to tears. This book became synonomous with the suffering of the Cape rebel.

Over the years, a wrong perception has been formed about the information in *Hoe Zij Stierven*. It was thought that this unique publication only dealt with the executions of Cape rebels; that only 32 of the 40 burgers executed were in fact Cape rebels seems to have been overlooked. In fact Scheepers, Liebenberg, Breed and Baxter were Republican burgers, while Toy and Veenstra were foreigners. Davis and Bester were deserters from the British armed forces. These eight names do not appear in the Government Blue Book, which lists the rebels who were executed in the Cape Colony.

Also unknown to many people is that there were at least 22 burgers who died before firing squads or on the gallows in the Republics during this period. Some were tried by Military Courts, while many died without any trial at all.

The fact that so little information was available about these executions was due to the military attitude that prevailed at the time. They simply brushed these affairs under the carpet and, in some cases, destroyed the evidence.

As a result, there is very little official information available about these trials and executions.[1]

After the war, the well-known British historian Arthur Conan Doyle took the trouble to compile a list of the executed, but he could find only a few examples in the Republics. He surmised that there could be more and states, 'but I can find no record of them, and if they exist at all, they must be few in number'. His list comprises only three in Pretoria, one in Johannesburg and one in Krugersdorp.[2]

The total executed was in fact much higher than Doyle could have anticipated. During January 1902, the commanding officer of the British forces in South Africa supplied a list of those executed in the Republics to the War Office in England. This list of 20 executed included the names of five black men and a burger, Dirk Breed, who was executed as a Cape rebel. We now arrive at a figure of 14 legitimate executions of burgers from the Republics according to that report.[3]

Thomas Pakenham, in his book *The Boer War*, mentions that there were 51 executions in all. If this number includes the 32 listed in the Government Blue Book as Cape rebels executed, then according to Pakenham only 11 died in the Republics.[4]

Because of faulty and defective records, the precise total of those executed in the Republics might never be known. However, from available records we have found at least 22 persons who were executed after being tried in court. These cases are dealt with in Section 2 as well as 24 other scandalous executions without trial.

Much information about executions in the Transvaal and Free State still lie hidden in archives, commemorative brochures, old newspapers and private correspondence.

Although much research has been done about the executions in the Cape Colony, and is still continuing, the executions in the Republics deserve further attention by historians, as this is one of the most neglected aspects of the Anglo-Boer War.[6]

Chapter 1

The Plot to Abduct Roberts

Hans Cordua (23)[1]
Executed by firing squad at Pretoria on 24 August 1900.

Hans Cordua had a masterplan to either murder or abduct Lord Roberts and senior British officers that would 'stagger Europe' if it succeeded. It would paralyse the British war effort in South Africa. These were the thoughts of this idealistic young German immigrant.

Cordua immigrated to the Transvaal three years before the outbreak of the war and advanced to lieutenant in the ZAR State Artillery. When Lord Roberts occupied Pretoria during June 1900, Cordua took the oath of neutrality, but a month later commenced his far-fetched plot. The plan was to set fire to some buildings on the western side of Pretoria and then to arm certain parties. Regular police members and burgers who were on parole and had free passes would occupy the homes of Lord Roberts and prominent military officers. During the confusion caused by the fire, Roberts and the officers would be kidnapped and taken to the nearest Boer commando. It was alleged that this plot had the blessing of General Louis Botha and that other Boer generals were aware of it. This was never proved.

It appears that Cordua was influenced by one Gano, a former British secret agent of Spanish extraction, who had fallen from grace in British circles. He was keen to restore his pride and at the same time make a name for himself. Gano presented himself to Cordua as a Boer supporter in the service of the British. Gano bought the whisky and supplied

Cordua with a British uniform and a free pass to enable him to move about freely in Pretoria and surrounds. To enhance his plot, he approached various prominent Pretoria citizens. It later appeared that none of them became actively involved. Gano then betrayed Cordua to the authorities, who promptly arrested him and threw him in gaol. At the time of his arrest, he was wearing the British uniform with which Gano had so thoughtfully supplied him. Also in his possession were detailed plans of the plot. A map of Pretoria was found with details of all the prominent British officers' homes on it, as well as the complete plan of the house Roberts lived in.

Six other influential citizens were charged with being accomplices of Cordua and they soon all appeared in court. It was proved that they merely had knowledge of the plot but had not contributed to it in any way. Their testimony actually strengthened the Crown's case against Cordua instead of incriminating themselves. They had however broken their paroles, and were banished from Pretoria. At least 100 former Transvaal burgers and police involved with the case were exiled to Ceylon, but only Cordua paid with his life.

There were strong indications that there was another mastermind behind Gano. Cordua was a naive idealist and not a revolutionary, who became the victim of a plot to use him to get to those who had violated their paroles. Lord Roberts took the case very lightly and believed the plot would have had little chance of success.

Conan Doyle maintained that Cordua was executed for breaking of his oath of neutrality rather than for the plot itself. A short while after the arrest of Cordua, but before his trial, Lord Roberts issued a proclamation warning that violation of the oath of neutrality was a serious offence and that offenders would be treated severely and could also qualify for the death sentence. The mastermind behind the plot was never discovered.

Cordua was condemned to death by a Military Court on 21 August for violating his oath of neutrality and for the conspiracy. Throughout his trial he appeared calm and unconcerned and displayed no emotion at all. Upon hearing his sentence he left the court proudly and upright. On 24 August Cordua perished before a firing squad in the garden of the Pretoria gaol and was buried there. As was the custom in the Cape Colony, he was seated on a chair and blindfolded. His request not to be bound was granted. He left a letter wherein he stated that he had received a fair trial.

Cordua was later reburied in the old cemetery in Church Street West, Pretoria. The inscription on his grave simply states:

Hans Cordua

Born 25 September 1876.

Died 24 August 1900.

Several others would also pay the highest toll for breaking their oaths of neutrality.

CHAPTER 2

'The Sympathetic Hero and Martyr'

Advocate Cornelis Broeksma (38)[1]
Executed by firing squad in Johannesburg on 30 September 1901.

Cornelis Broeksma was a Dutch immigrant who was executed for incurring the wrath of the British by exposing the concentration camp atrocities in South Africa to Europe. After his death, he was honoured in Holland as a hero and martyr because of his extremely sympathetic stand regarding the Boers.

Cornelis Broeksma.
Photograph supplied by a
grandson of Broeksma, Reitz
Broeksma of Somerset West.

The decision taken by the Boers to continue with guerilla warfare after the fall of Pretoria resulted in intensive behind-the-scenes negotiations by diplomats. Many burgers who had signed the oath of neutrality returned to the commandos, while others spied on the British and supplied information to their brethren under arms. Because of this some were executed. The activity on the diplomatic front was mainly aimed at making the outside world aware of the concentration camps and the scorched-earth policy of the British, and thus gain support for the Boer cause. Cornelis Broeksma immersed himself in this cause heart and soul, sending secret coded messages to the Dutch ambassador.

The so-called triangular conspiracy, which was exposed towards the latter part of 1901, revolved around Dr WJ Leyds, the Republican ambassador in the Netherlands, and Dr FET Krause, the former Johannesburg chief prosecuter, and Advocate Cornelis Broeksma, the former public prosecutor from Johannesburg. After the occupation of Pretoria by the British, Dr Krause was replaced and placed on parole, but because of ill health was allowed to go to London. From London he corresponded in a secret code with Broeksma. Broeksma supplied him with up-to-date news regarding the scorched-earth policy atrocities as well as the latest mortality figures from the concentration camps. He obtained these figures in a clandestine fashion from official British statistics. He requested Krause to pass these on through diplomatic channels to Leyds in the Hague. Leyds was to make sure that they were passed on to other ambassadors.

From London, Krause informed Broeksma that a certain journalist in London, Douglas Forster, was causing great damage to their cause overseas. A letter from Forster had recently appeared in a British newspaper stating that all Boer prisoners should be executed because they were a bunch of freebooters! He also spread false information about British prisoners being gunned down in cold blood by the Boers. Although this information was rejected by Kitchener, he continued to describe the Boers as outright murderers. Krause wrote to Broeksma stating that something should be done about it and suggested, 'that they can shoot him or get rid of him in some manner'.[2]

This letter was intercepted by the American consul in Rotterdam and handed over to British intelligence. The code was deciphered and Krause was arrested in London and Broeksma in Johannesburg. Krause was first charged with high treason, but this was later changed to incitement to murder and breaking his oath of neutrality. He was sentenced to two years imprisonment in England and released in 1903.

When Broeksma arrived in South Africa, he continued with his law studies in Bloemfontein, becoming an advocate. With the outbreak of hostilities, he was appointed as deputy prosecuter in the office of the Advocate-General in Johannesburg. With the British occupation of Pretoria he was replaced and placed on parole because of his support for the Republics. The same happened to Krause.

The sheet music and lyrics of a song in honour of Broeksma, which was published in the Dutch newspaper Timotheus.
Source: Reitz Broeksma, grandson of Advocate Cornelis Broeksma

Broeksma immediately became involved in the commission of Dutch churches, which monitored the concentration-camp situation in Johannesburg very closely and which also gave support in aid. His charitable work soon aroused the suspicion of the British intelligence service. After the interception of his coded messages to Dr Krause in England his house was raided and searched. A large collection of documents was found as well as information about the concentration camps. The connection with Leyds in the Hague was now uncovered. In fact all that had been discovered was the zeal of Broeksma to expose the atrocious conditions of the concentration camps to the people of Europe. He was summarily charged with breaking his oath of neutrality, treason and incitement with regard to the violation of the oath.

With his knowledge of the law, Broeksma pleaded guilty to all the charges. On 14 September 1901 he was found guilty and sentenced to death, which was ratified by Kitchener. On 30 September he died before a firing squad at the Johannesburg Fort and was buried in the garden. According to a letter from the Advocate-General of the Transvaal, permission was granted to exhume his body in 1909 for reburial. While this was being carried out, the remains of two other burgers, Vermaak and Wernick, were discovered in the garden. More of them in a later chapter.

Broeksma was honoured as a hero and martyr in Holland. A postcard of him and his family was issued in the Netherlands after his execution. He was described as: 'The sympathetic hero and martyr.' An original postcard is in the possession of Mr CA Hollenbach of Florida Park who is a collector of Anglo-Boer War letters, and kindly supplied us with a copy for publication.

In September 1901, the Netherlands newspaper *Timotheus* issued an eulogy about Broeksma. The facts about Broeksma emerged mainly from this source because of the lack of official documentation available. At a later date, *Timotheus* also printed sheet music in ballad form honouring Broeksma. After the war, a Netherlands organisation took care of his widow and four small children because the family had lost everything and they were destitute. The organisation approached the Attorney-General of the Transvaal to have Broeksma reburied in the Braamfontein cemetery, chosen because of the high costs involved at the Johannesburg cemetery.

Over the years, all records of the grave of Cornelis Broeksma were

A photograph taken of Broeksma's grave and tombstone in about 1909 after a Dutch organisation had erected it in the cemetery at Braamfontein. The grave of one 'Golding' in the background led to the rediscovery of the grave in 1997.
Photograph: Reitz Broeksma, Somerset West

Mr Reitz Broeksma, a grandson of Cornelis Broeksma, at the grave that was only found after a protracted search.
Photograph: Reitz Broeksma, Somerset West

lost. The register of graves at the Braamfontein cemetery revealed nothing. In 1997 a grandson of Broeksma, Reitz Broeksma, a surveyor from Somerset West, was successful in finding his grave, with the aid of an old photograph taken at the reburial.[3]

While Gideon Scheepers was a martyr to truth and justice in the Cape Colony, Cornelis Broeksma was a martyr to charity in the Transvaal.

This photograph appears on a postcard issued in honour of Broeksma in 1902. The subtitle reads: 'Held en martelaar voor de barmhartigheid' (Hero and martyr for compassion).
Source: CA Hollenbach, Florida Park

CHAPTER 3

Murder Under the White Flag and After Surrender

Field-Cornet Salmon van As (24)[1]
Executed by firing squad at Heidelberg on 23 June 1902.

By September 1901, many Boers in the Eastern Transvaal were laying down their arms because they were losing heart in the struggle and the conditions that their families had to endure in the concentration camps. Near a British fort at De Kuilen, approximately 19 kilometres south of

Assistant field-cornet Salmon van As.
Photograph received from Mr Hannes
Hattingh of Verwoerdburg – nephew of
Salmon van As.

Heidelberg, a Boer patrol was scouting and never returned. The Boers received reports that a British officer had approached the patrol under a white flag. Further information revealed that this officer had come with gifts and promises and had convinced the burgers to go over to the British. He told them that it was unnecessary for women and children to die in the camps as their cause was already lost.

On 25 September, Field-Cornet Salmon van As, accompanied by Louis Slabbert and Piet du Toit, were sent out to capture a party of

188

*The artist AC Ball's depiction of the meeting between Captain Miers and
Field-Cornet Van As.*
Copied from After Pretoria, *by Wilson*

Boers who were heading in the direction of the fort to surrender, and, better still, to trap the British officer who was causing these defections. They hid their horses and approached the fort on foot until they were visible to the soldiers manning the fort. They could clearly see the British watching them through binoculars.

During the early afternoon a British officer on horseback approached slowly. There was later conflicting evidence given as to which party had carried a white flag, Van As or the British officer. One thing, however, is certain and that is that there was a white flag visible, because the officer rode up to Van As without any party closing for action. When the officer was about 300 paces away, Van As ordered Slabbert to approach unarmed and warn the officer not to come any closer to their observation post. The officer, armed with a revolver, ignored Slabbert's order and rode on towards Van As. Captain Miers was clearly under the impression that Van As and his colleagues had come to surrender, while Van As was convinced that he had found the man who was talking the Boers into surrendering. Van As did not want to give his rifle to Miers and an argument began about who was surrendering to whom. Miers reached for his revolver but Van As was quicker, and the officer tumbled from his horse, shot through the heart.

Upon his return to his commando, Van As reported the incident to his commandant, who viewed it as an ordinary war occurrence. General Botha was of the opinion that the case should be brought before a Boer Military Court, but the overwhelming feeling was that Van As had acted in self-defence. The case was never heard, and this was to cost Van As dearly, as it meant that the British could now charge Van As with murder.

The British military authorities never forgot this incident. During the peace negotiations, the British made three exclusions regarding the amnesty of burgers. One being Salmon van As. When General Botha informed Van As of this, he answered that if his life could not be guaranteed he would ride to South-West Africa, as he still had two good horses. Botha assured him that he had nothing to fear from a possible enquiry, and he rode in and surrendered. This cost him his life, as nothing came from the assurances of Botha.

On 8 June, Salmon van As and Louis Slabbert were asked to report to the British military authorities. They were immediately placed under arrest and tried by a Military Court at Middelburg on 17 June. By arresting Slabbert, Kitchener broke his solemn undertaking that only Van As, Commandant Celliers and the burger Muller would be excluded from amnesty and that all other burgers would not be brought to court after peace was declared.[2] The arrest of Slabbert was possibly the reason why Commandant Conroy fled to Europe, as he did not want to find himself in the same situation.

For being an accomplice to murder, Slabbert was sentenced to life imprisonment. This was later reduced to five years, and when a general amnesty was declared in 1903 he was released. Van As received the death sentence for the murder of Captain Ronald Miers of the Somersets.

As was the case in so many trials of this nature, the evidence of black witnesses was heard in court. In this instance, a group was called in from a nearby mission station to testify against Van As and Slabbert. Van As had to conduct his own defence in English, which was difficult to say the least. Slabbert was not asked to testify as he could not understand a word of English. All records of this trial have disappeared.

Two years after the war, the British authorities apologised to the parents of Salmon van As and offered compensation. They admitted that false witnesses had been used from the mission station during the case against their son. The Van As family rejected the compensation outright because: 'The blood of our son will not be bought by money.' To this day, the trial of Van As is a contentious matter.

On 23 June 1902, the young Boer officer was taken to the rear of the stone prison and placed with his back to the wall. He refused to be blindfolded. A volley from the Somerset's firing squad avenged the death of their popular young officer. Van As was rolled into a blanket and buried in a shallow grave about 600 paces away along the road to the old cemetery on the Sugarbush Ridge. Field-Cornet Hans Botha later planted a thorn tree over the temporary grave so that people would know where he lay. He was reburied on 13 October 1903 in the old cemetery at Heidelberg. On 12 March 1938, a statue was unveiled honouring seven burgers from Heidelberg who died during this war. One of the names included on it is that of Salmon van As.

> Beside the churchyard's ringwall,
> Here in the clay-hard sand,
> There grows a lonely thorn tree,
> A thirteen year old plant,
> It guards an empty grave spot,
> Under the Sugarbushrand.

C Louis Leipoldt[3]

Pieter (Piet) Schuil (23)[4]
Executed by firing squad in the Rustenburg district on 2 October 1901.

Piet Schuil was captured on 30 September 1901 during the mauling of a column commanded by Colonel Kekewich. General Kemp fell upon the British at Moedwil, 15 kilometres west of Rustenburg, where the road crossed the Selons River. A skirmish followed but the Boers had to retreat because of accurate cannon fire directed at them by the British.

Schuil did not take part in the fighting because he was part of the detail appointed to guard the horses. During the confusion of the Boer withdrawal, the horses broke loose and Schuil found himself alone. He

Piet Schuil. This photograph was originally published in Schröder-Nielsen's book Onder die Boere in Vrede en Oorlog *published in Oslo in 1925 and was borrowed from* Historia *of May 1977.*

remained sitting on the bank of the Selons River. He was too far from the Boer commando to flee on foot, so he decided to surrender.

According to Schuil, he tied a piece of white cloth to the barrel of his rifle and held it aloft so as to be clearly visible to the approaching troops. His evidence was confirmed by a burger who was captured close by, but two British troopers swore under oath that he had fired upon them while the white cloth was still tied to his rifle.

Schuil was tried at a military sitting at the British camp at Moedwil on 1 October and notified that he would be executed the following day. The testimony of the burger captured near to him was rejected and he was refused permission to call in his defence his close friend, Schroder-Nielsen, who was also captured during the skirmish. That night they were bound hand and foot and placed under guard in a tent.

Both these men had immigrated to South Africa in 1898 and settled in the Transvaal. Schuil was a well-qualified teacher and gave lessons at Rietvlei near Rustenburg before the war.

With the outbreak of hostilities, he was conscripted into the commandos. It appears that he was more interested in literature than warfare, because he was usually occupied with poetry and readings from Heinrich Heine. There is a possibility that because of this attitude he was detailed to guard the horses at Moedwil rather than to participate in the battle.

His friend Peter Ingvald Schroder-Nielsen was a Norwegian assistant surveyor from Rustenburg who lived on a smallholding on the outskirts of the town. When his house was plundered by the British, he left and joined the commando of General Koos de la Rey. During the evenings around the campfires, these two inseparable friends sat and discussed poetry and read. Nielsen is to be thanked for the information he left about his friend's capture and execution. Without his contribution, this incident would have been conveniently swept under the carpet. This narrative appears in the book *With the Boers in Peace and Conflict*,* published in Oslo in 1925.

The letters that Schuil wrote to his parents before his execution never reached them. Nielsen offered to publish his friend's novels and poems, which were buried somewhere near Rustenburg, but Schuil was not at all interested, and the writings and poems of this young dreamer have never seen the light of day.

The following morning before sunrise, he was led to an open grave. Nielsen accompanied him. He was placed on a chair behind a small brick dwelling on the banks of the Selons River. He refused the brandy offered to him and objected to being blindfolded.

'You are a brave man', the officer remarked; 'I cannot believe that you are guilty.'

Schuil answered in a clear voice: 'I am innocent, but I do not want to exchange my place with those two soldiers who under oath swore falsely against me.'

While Schuil was reading his Bible, the morning stillness was shattered by a fusillade from the firing squad. Pages from the Bible flew into the air. Schroder-Nielsen was ordered to appear before a major and given an ultimatum. He could become a spy for the British, or he would be tried for shooting at a wounded officer, which could carry the death sentence. If he became a spy, the charges against him would be dropped. Nielsen refused to cooperate and enquired indignantly whether he was sitting among a bunch of murderers or the prisoner of war of a civilised nation.

The accusations against him were set aside in Pretoria, possibly because of his Norwegian citizenship, as Britain was on friendly terms with that country. He was subsequently banished to Bermuda.

*(*Brand boerne i fred op krig*)

On 10 October 1934, the remains of Schuil and other burgers were exhumed along the banks of the Selons River and reburied on the farm Dwarsspruit near Rustenburg. An obelisk was later erected over the new graves and on it appear the names of 10 burgers, one of them that of Piet Schuil.

His name also appears on the rolls of honour to be found on the church walls of the Dutch Reformed churches in Bloemfontein and Pretoria. These are the names of 78 men from the Netherlands who sacrificed their lives for the Boer cause during the war.

Jan Abraham Basson
TC Lombard
PC Fourie
Executed by firing squad at Frederikstad station on 27 October 1900.

Some 300 paces from the small railway siding of Frederikstad, just to the north of Potchefstroom, stands a monument in memory of the Boers who fell in battle there. Not all were killed in that encounter; three were executed after it ended.

In October 1900, General de Wet trapped a large British column under General Burton at Frederikstad. He kept the British under siege and called for assistance from commandos operating in the Western Transvaal. When the reinforcements did not arrive, De Wet was compelled to retreat. The British pursued him and in the process the Boers suffered heavily. Apart from their 30 casualties, many were captured during De Wet's biggest setback of the war.[5]

Among the prisoners were three Boers who were accused of firing at the British after they had surrendered. An officer was killed. They were immediately tried by a military hearing and summarily shot.

The burger Marais, who was captured at the same time, recalled in his memoirs that a few Boers took shelter in a ditch during the retreat.[6]

The British were advancing so fast that they did not notice the group of Boers. From the ditch they killed a number of soldiers as they sped by. Their position was discovered and a skirmish commenced during which they suffered some wounded. They then decided to surrender. One of the Boers threw his hands into the air and was promptly shot by an officer. Jan Basson grabbed his rifle and shot the officer. Three of them

194

Pretoria.

Dear Sir,

I regret to say that J.A.
Basson was one of 3 men shot
at Freidrickstadt on Oct 26 for
surrendering, and then shooting
again after our men had passed.
I am

Yours faithfully

R.M.Powerley
Provost Marshal

A photocopy of the letter sent to Basson's father to inform him that his son
had been executed.
Source: Mrs. JA Killian, Paarl

were charged with treacherous conduct and the murder of the officer. A letter from Basson to his betrothed before his execution has been preserved by the family. The paper is very flimsy and falling apart, but reads:

Frederikstad,
26 October 1900

My dearest Joe,
I must say my last farewell to you – tomorrow morning I am to be shot. An English military court has sentenced me to death. I cannot describe to you how painful the thought is of the pain that you must endure for my sake. I hope that it will give you some comfort to know that I die in the belief of a just God who will be merciful towards me, and that we might meet again someday in Heaven.
Your everlasting, understanding sweetheart,

Jan Basson

The three executed men and the Boers who died in the battle were buried in a communal trench. After the war they were reburied in the small cemetery near the station and a monument was erected in their honour. The names of the 41 appear on this monument, but due to weathering and vandalism the names of the three executed are not legible.[7] The Roberts Papers, which are kept at the Transvaal Archives, do record the battle at Frederikstad but make no mention of the three Boers who were executed. According to a list issued by the commanding officer of the British forces in January 1902, the three executed Boers were TC Lombard, PC Fourie and JA Basson.[8]

CHAPTER 4

Murder

Christiaan Lodewicus Pienaar (17)
Hanged at Bloemfontein on 1 November 1900.

Years after the war, the following notice appeared in *Die Volksblad:*[1] 'The following is a copy of the last letter written by the young Pienaar from the prison in Bloemfontein where he was condemned to death by the Military Authorities. Upon the evidence given by kaffirs, he and his brother and father had murdered an English officer.'

The shortened version of the translation is as follows:

Bloemfontein
12 October 1900
Mrs DMS Pienaar,
Nooitgedacht.

Loving and dearest Mother,
I sent a message for you to visit me with the Provost Marshall, who asked if I wanted to see anybody else, but it now looks as if you cannot come. Therefore I am writing to let you know that everything is fine with me and I hope that everything is going well with you.

Dearest mother, I have been condemned to death because of the false evidence given by our labourers. Our Lord Jesus also had to carry His burden in all innocence and therefore I am happy with my lot. This I do know: God does not sleep. He sees everything. It is the lot of a person to die only once and then comes the judgement.

Oh! my dear mother, I am more concerned about you and father and my brothers and sisters than I am of myself.

I am going to leave this world with all its troubles, worries and sins. I am going to say farewell to it all and cast my eyes upon the mountains, from whence cometh my help. My help is from the Lord.

Dearest Mother, be not distressed. Ask the Lord to give you strength and guidance, which He will certainly do ...

Signed: CL Pienaar.

He further urges his family to prepare themselves for the long journey to eternity because the day will come when they all have to meet God. He also urges M to be obedient and his mother not to grieve anymore.

On 25 September 1900, the young Pienaar was found guilty of murder in the first degree by the Military Court in Bloemfontein. He was to hang for the death of a British officer, one Wilson. The execution was carried out in the Bloemfontein gaol on 1 November. His father, Willem Pienaar, and his brother Salomon were both found guilty of second-degree murder and received life sentences. The authorities refused to hand over the body to the family.[2]

The incident had taken place towards the end of August when Commandant Haasbroek cornered the British at Helpmekaar, in the Winburg district. While the skirmish was still in progress, two of Pienaar's cousins, Roedolf and Andries Pienaar, both members of the commando, were given permission to pay a short visit to his family farm to enquire as to the welfare of the family.

Seventeen-year-old Christiaan Pienaar, who was hanged in Bloemfontein. Photograph taken from Dagbreek en Landstem *submitted by Mr CL Pienaar of Kragbron*

When they approached the farmhouse, Salomon, Christiaan's younger brother, came out to warn them that there was an English spy in the house and that they should come back after he had departed.

Roedolf and Andries turned their horses around and left. While they were riding past the dam, Andries said that it was their duty to shoot or take the officer prisoner because it was war and they were still on commando. They then dismounted and hid behind the dam wall and waited for the officer, who had to pass that way.

A short while later the officer appeared, in uniform and armed. They shouted for him to halt, but he refused to do so, and they both opened fire. Roedolf's rifle jammed but Andries shot him out of his saddle. They took his boots and saddle and found a handkerchief in his inside pocket. On it was the name Wilson.

On the road back to the house, they found Christiaan at the water pump on the banks of the river, working with the farm labourers. They told him of the incident and all returned to the farmhouse. The entire family, including Willem, Salomon and Christiaan, went and buried the officer.

One of the black labourers later defected to the British and became a spy for them. He reported the incident and told the authorities that his master had shot the officer. Because Roedolf and Andries were back on commando, Christiaan was taken into custody by a British column and charged with the murder of Wilson. His father and brother were also apprehended and charged as accomplices. The court heard Christiaan explain that he had nothing to do with the murder and he was busy with the pump at the river at the time. The court refused to believe his testimony and accepted the evidence of the labourer instead. Christiaan was executed and Willem and Salomon received life sentences.

When Roedolf and Andries returned from exile after the war, the truth became known. In sworn affidavits both Roedolf and Andries took full responsibility for the shooting of Wilson. They stated that the death shot was fired by Andries and that Christiaan was nowhere near at the time of the shooting.

On 25 October 1902, Mrs Pienaar requested the release of her husband and young son on the grounds of this new evidence. The Colonial Secretary in Bloemfontein received both her plea and the sworn affidavits. After lengthy negotiations with the Colonial Secretary, as well as with the Lord Chamberlain, she eventually received an answer. Their findings were that although the sworn affidavits might be true, they did not alter the fact that Willem and Salomon were guilty of being participants in the crime. However, the 'unusual circumstances' surrounding the case enabled them to reduce their sentences of five to seven years' imprisonment. According to the Pienaar family, the authorities later acknowledged that the Military Court had erred, and as compensation, Mrs Pienaar received a lifelong grant from the British.

No official records of this tragedy can be found. Details are however to be found in the letters of Mrs Pienaar pleading for clemency for her loved ones. The full story of this family disaster appeared on 12 October 1969 in the *Dagbreek en Landstem*, in an article by Christiaan Lodewicus Pienaar, the son of Roedolf. Mr Pienaar, who lives at Kragbron, further related that his father swore on Christiaan's grave to seek vengeance against the black man upon whose evidence his brother was executed. Some time later, while out scouting, Roedolf came upon the man, dressed in uniform, and shot him immediately.

Mr Pienaar later obtained a copy of Christiaan's letter written from his death cell, the same letter that appeared years after the war in *Die Volksblad*. He received the copy and a photo of Christiaan from a reader in Salisbury who sent them to the newspaper.

The long search by the family for the grave of Christiaan has resulted in failure.

Jacobus Johannes de Jager[3]
Hanged at Harrismith on 18 March 1901.

On 14 February 1901, two Boers, Jacobus Johannes de Jager of Southeyshoek and a certain Snyman from Bethlehem in the district of Harrismith, fell into British hands. De Jager appeared before a Military Court in Harrismith, charged with the murder of three black men. According to letters written by De Jager from his death cell, it appears that Snyman turned Crown witness. His evidence resulted in the conviction of De Jager. Snyman testified that on 8 December 1900 De Jager shot a black man named Mooikaffer and a youngster named Frans while they were herding cattle. The second charge against De Jager was that he shot a black man named Klasie, alias April, on 11 February 1901.

Because this hearing was conducted behind closed doors little is known about the case itself. It is not certain whether De Jager had legal representation or not. His family later declared that his defence was that blacks were not considered combatants and were shot because they were on the side of the enemy.

No records of this case can be found, but the information is based on a report that appeared in the *Harrismith News* of 22 March 1901. According to the article, De Jager admitted to the shooting, but nobody could actually verify this.

The Military Court under the presidency of Lieutenant-Colonel Pratt sentenced De Jager to death on 19 February. Kitchener confirmed the sentence and De Jager was hanged in the gaol at Harrismith on 18 March. That evening he was buried outside the cemetery on the eastern side.

Commandant RD van Schalkwyk
Executed by firing squad at Krugersdorp on 17 December 1901.

Van Schalkwyk was from the farm Hartebeesfontein in the Krugersdorp district. At a hearing on 8 December 1901, he was charged with treason and shooting a wounded soldier after capture. He was sentenced to death and executed on 26 December at Krugersdorp.[4] After the war, his widow lodged a claim against the British for their destruction of the farmhouse and outbuildings as well as the confiscation of belongings. Her claim amounted to £3018, which indicates that her husband was a successful farmer. In her claim, she stated that her husband was executed, but she 'did not know what for'.

The reply to her claim was:

'Amount allowed: Nil.

'Remarks: Disallowed. Husband was tried at Krugersdorp in Dec. 1901 and executed.'[5]

These happenings demonstrate the secrecy that surround these trials and the scarcity of available information.

Jan Lewis (46)
Executed by firing squad at Potchefstroom on 14 October 1901.

Lewis was a widower who left six children behind as well as having all his property and farm destroyed during the war. He appeared before the Military Court on 30 September 1901 in Potchefstroom on a charge of murder. He was executed on 14 October. His death notice was inscribed by J Swart on 20 January 1902 at the Potchefstroom concentration camp.[6]

CHAPTER 5

Captured in Khaki

SJ (Fransie) Kruger (20)[1]
Executed by firing squad at Frankfort on 29 January 1902.

Towards the end of January 1902, the Heidelberg commando was forced into the Free State and joined up with the Frankfort commando. They were in tatters and their horses were spent.

The commando now consisted of about 300 men and they received news that a column of Kitchener's scouts had overrun one of their outlying posts and captured Field-Cornet Strydom. They immediately set after the column and intercepted them at Damplaats, across the Wilge River. A running battle followed and continued for a day. Strydom was freed and the British lost eight men, with 16 badly wounded and 170 taken prisoner. The Heidelbergers then helped themselves to the scouts' uniforms. The Boers were under strict orders to discard all military buttons and badges found on uniforms. The British soldiers were compelled to wear the tatters of their captors. They were marched back to Frankfort by their major, who was allowed to keep his uniform.

The commando now made its way towards the Vaal River for a much-needed rest. This was not to be, as one of General French's flying columns pounced on them shortly afterwards. Many of the Boers had not had time to remove the insignia from the British uniforms they now wore. When the alarms was given, Fransie Kruger, an epileptic, suffered an attack brought about by the shock appearance of the British. His father refused to leave him and they were both captured. Fransie was taken to Frankfort where he was found guilty of wearing a British uniform and executed. His father, Gert, pleaded in vain for his son's life. It is not known where Fransie lies buried.

Three more Boers were executed in the Republics during the war for wearing captured uniforms.[2] The location of the farms where these executions took place has not been established, and no further information has been found.

I Koen
Executed by firing squad at Jakkalsfontein on 15 April 1902.
Transvaal

Straus (Struis)
Executed by firing squad at Vlakfontein on 24 December 1901.
Free State

C Steyn
Executed by firing squad at Blouboschspruit on 21 January 1902.
Free State

CHAPTER 6

Oath Violation and High Treason

After the capture of Bloemfontein and Pretoria, the two Boer Republics were annexed by Britain. The inhabitants were thus legally British subjects and Boers still under arms were therefore rebels. Lord Roberts speedily instructed the courts that any burger captured should be tried as a rebel. This was completely indefensible as many Boers were still involved in the war and on commando. Furthermore, it was contradictory to international law. When captured, burgers were still classified as prisoners of war. Those who laid down their arms had to take an oath of neutrality, which meant they were actually prisoners on parole.[1]

It was to become obvious that the Boers did not take the oath of neutrality serious. Many returned to their commandos and others became involved in activities to undermine the occupying authorities. When recaptured, they were charged with oath violation and high treason. With the execution of Hans Cordua during August 1900, Roberts gave notice of his intentions to deal strictly with oath violations. They could, in fact, receive the death penalty.

PR Krause
NT Venter[2]
Executed by firing squad at Pretoria on 11 June 1901.

Early in June 1901, six Boers who had taken the oath of neutrality and were on parole in Pretoria made an effort to rejoin their commando.

They got as far as the Pietersburg railway station where they encountered a police patrol, and a shoot-out followed. A policeman was injured and the three were taken captive.

On 10 June, Krause, Venter and Delport appeared in court at Pretoria, charged with attempted murder, breaking the oath of neutrality and the unlawful possession of firearms. Krause was found guilty on all three charges, while Venter and Delport were found guilty on charges two and three. All three were condemned to death. Delport received clemency because of his age and was held as a prisoner of war, while Krause and Venter were executed in Pretoria prison. Krause and Venter, like Cordua, were originally buried in the prison garden. According to records in the Transvaal Archives, the Attorney-General gave permission in 1909 for relatives to exhume the remains of the two men. Their graves were found under a small zinc building in the yard of the Pretoria fire brigade.[3] There is a possibility that they were reburied, like Cordua, in the old Church Street cemetery in Pretoria West. Their graves have not been found.

David Garnus Wernick (37)[4]
Executed by firing squad at Johannesburg on 19 November 1901.

Wernick, a father of five children, was a born Cape colonial from Beaufort West and, therefore, British. He was interned at the camp in Johannesburg where he encouraged captive Boers to go back and fight. His actions annoyed the authorities to such an extent that they had him arrested. On 2 November 1901, he appeared before a Military Court, charged with breaking the oath of neutrality, inciting persons to break the oath and high treason. He may have been tried as a Cape rebel because he was not a Transvaal citizen. He was found guilty and executed in the Johannesburg Fort on 19 November and buried in the adjoining garden.

With the exhumation of Cornelis Broeksma's remains in 1909, it was confirmed that two more men were buried in the garden, namely Wernick and Vermaak. Records of the Attorney-General tend to confirm that they were reburied elsewhere.

Renier Christiaan Upton (34)[5]
Executed by firing squad at Pretoria on 21 August 1901.

Upton, a 34-year-old farmer, was a born Cape colonial from Hangklip, Queenstown, and held British citizenship. It is possible that he could have been tried as a Cape rebel. He appeared in court on 13 August 1901 in Pretoria, charged with spying. He was found guilty and faced the firing squad on 21 August. Upton could also have been reburied during 1909 with Cordua, Krause and Venter in the old Church Street cemetery in Pretoria West.

Vermaak[6]
Executed by firing squad at Johannesburg during October 1901.

A burger named Vermaak was executed on the 'authority from the military' in the Old Fort at Johannesburg during October 1901. This meant that he was tried by a Military Court, possibly for an oath violation. His remains were found in the garden during the exhumation of Cornelis Broeksma, who was buried in a coffin. Vermaak had no coffin. This information was given by the Attorney-General's office in 1909 during the exhumation of Broeksma's remains. Other than this 'acknowledgement' from the Attorney-General's office, no further information was made public regarding the execution of Vermaak. Vermaak's reburial place is unknown. It may be presumed that other executions took place of which the public were kept in complete ignorance.

CHAPTER 7

The Execution of a Deserter – A Love Story

Trooper George Frederick Shaw[1]
Executed by firing squad at Ventersdorp in June 1902.

If you ever pass through the little hamlet of Ventersdorp, and you have some time on your hands, go into the little cemetery, and there, quite close to the northwestern wall, you will see the solitary iron military cross of G Shaw. The disc reads as follows: 'For King and Empire. Pte G Shaw. 1st Loyal North Lancs.' There is no date of death mentioned. Fifty paces to the south lie other British graves, but Shaw's stands alone; and here's the reason why.

George Frederick Shaw, of Irish descent, joined the British Army and was posted out to the Western Transvaal, serving under Lord Methuen. He was a young man at the time, and fell in love with a Boer girl by the name of Martha Engelbrecht. This relationship was progressing nicely until the declaration by Kitchener, after the fall of Bloemfontein and Pretoria, that if the Boer forces did not surrender, the British would burn down their farmsteads and intern all Boer women and children in camps.

As fate would have it, it was Shaw's regiment that was ordered to burn Martha's farm. When the troops arrived and gave the customary 10 minutes to gather up their belongings, Martha fell upon upon her knees in front of her lover, and with tears streaming down her cheeks beseeched him not to destroy her home. Shaw refused to torch the homestead, and he and his companions returned to camp.

The commanding officer, on hearing what had transpired, had a stand-up row with Shaw, and in the heat of the argument said, 'Well Shaw, if that's the way you feel, why don't you join the Boers?'

That night, under darkness, Shaw left the camp, buried his British uniform, and joined the Boers. He got a job as an unarmed transport rider and moved into Martha's house.

The Boers eventually surrendered, and Shaw, who had grown a beard and was dressed in Boer clothes, was taken along with other prisoners to the Ventersdorp station to be railed off to a concentration camp. On the platform the prisoners were lined up to receive rations when Shaw, being a trained British soldier, made the fatal error of snapping to attention!

The sergeant on duty immediately said, 'That's no Boer, that's a Tommy!' and Shaw was arrested. They found out who he was, and he was court martialled for desertion. Shaw was found guilty and marched to the old cemetery, where he had to pace off 50 paces to the north, so that he would not be buried in consecrated ground, given a pick and shovel, and told to dig his own grave. They tied him to a chair, which is in the possession of his descendants in Klerksdorp, blindfolded him, and a firing squad was marched up.

It is said that they missed on the first round, in protest or as punishment, but the command was given once again, and Shaw tumbled backwards into his grave.

The grave of Private Shaw, the deserter who fought with the Boers, under the high, dead bluegum tree in the cemetery at Ventersdorp. Photograph: Hans Strydom, Brits

CHAPTER 8

Executions
Without Trial

Breaker Morant and the Bushveld Carbineers

The executions previously described were approved by the Military Courts set up under martial law, which was promulgated after the annexation of the two Republics and described as 'the will of the conqueror'.[1] The thesis of Dr JH Snyman, *Rebel trials in the Cape Colony during the Second War of Independence, with special reference to Military Courts, (1899–1902)** reveals a certain confusion among the British authorities regarding martial law.

Judge J Solomon stated: 'The subject of martial law is certainly one of considerable obscurity. However, once proclaimed it tends to stand. Martial law takes effect when the legal proceedings of a country cannot guarantee safety within its present structure. The reason for martial law is to effectively grant the State extraordinary power and regulations to once again guarantee law and order within its society. We may therefore look upon martial law as the law of necessity in the face of a grave emergency.' As such, the object was thus not to administer law with justice, although the condemned were usually given a hearing.

Many civilians and commando members were executed in cold blood without any hearings at all.[2] To speak of such proceedings as trials can be entirely misleading. In the words of CJ Cockburn: 'Martial Law

* *Rebelle Verhoor in Kaapstad gedurend die Tweede Vryheidsoorlog met Spesiale verwysing na Militere Howe (1899–1902).* Dr JH Snyman.

209

is a shadowy, uncertain, precarious something, depending entirely on the conscience, or rather on the despotic and arbitary will of those who administer it. Thus the commanding officer has total authority under Martial Law and his action is only limited by the necessity of adhering to the recognised laws and customs of war, and of using with discretion the exceptional powers given him. It is thus difficult to picture any legitimate warlike operation or measure which while war is raging in England, a Commander can order and command what he pleases and can inflict any punishment'.*

Executions without trial must therefore be classed as murder. How should we classify the cold-blooded shooting of a captive or civilian by a soldier who had received orders from higher command? In many instances, there was not enough evidence available to differentiate between execution and murder.

For example, there was the incident where Jan Muller, his two sons and other civilians were killed by black troops at Loskop in the Bethlehem district on 20 October 1901.[3] John Grobler was captured and summarily executed because he had been the cause of the death of two English officers during an ambush near Witbank.[4] However, in the shocking massacre of Boer civilians by black troops under the command of English officers at Holkrans and Derdepoort, one may be able to tell the difference between a skirmish, execution and murder.[5]

In the faraway regions of the Bushveld and the Northern Transvaal, gruesome executions of burgers and Boer civilians took place. Only after some foreigners were murdered by Australian troops did the British authorities deem it fit to intervene, thus avoiding a diplomatic confrontation with the country concerned.[6]

The war in the far regions of the Western and Northern Transvaal now took on a new dimension. It became a struggle between Boers and black troops commanded by British officers.[7] General Kemp sent a strongly worded letter of protest to Colonel Kekewich wherein he detailed executions of Boer prisoners who were later found with their skulls smashed in. Kemp warned that he had issued orders to the effect that any black soldier captured by the Boers would be executed because they had been armed by the British. He also drew Kekewich's attention

* Chapter 1 of the thesis by Dr JH Snyman.

210

to a shocking attack by them upon a laager of women and children.[8] General Smuts wrote to President Kruger: 'A pen cannot describe the suffering of the woman heroes of our nation ... fleeing away from the enemy between the bushes and mountains of Rustenburg, Waterberg, Zoutpansberg, Lydenburg, Swaziland and Zululand where the many white bones call upon heaven to deliver them from the barbaric blacks and even more barbaric British.'[9]

After the war Boer commanders took statements from persons who witnessed these violations of human rights. NC Havenga, the Adjutant-Secretary to General Hertzog, collected more than 100 of these declarations of atrocities.[10]

These documents were only to become interesting items in the Archives, as at the Peace of Vereeniging it was forbidden for any person serving in the British forces to be brought to trial for deeds committed during the conflict. The Cape Parliament was quick to follow suit, passing a Bill whereby it exonerated the British military authorities from any unlawful act committed during the war.[11]

Although a general amnesty was granted to the Republican burgers at the peace conference, it was declared that three would face trial. Furthermore, the Cape rebels would still have to face trial for alleged war crimes. The only guarantee was that they would not be liable for the death sentence. Rebel trials continued well into 1903, and many suffered and died during their internment in the various gaols throughout the regions before the doors were thrown open in a general amnesty for all.[12]

Britain never had to take the stand in a court to defend herself against war-crime allegations. To the victor, only the vanquished were sinners. What follows is the saga of two Australians executed by the British as scapegoats for the hideous conduct of British troops in general. These executions of their own troops were intended to demonstrate that the British military authorities were just and fair in their attitude towards war crimes.

Lieutenant Henry Morant's Bushveld Carbineers[13]

During an orgy of murder by this unit, 24 Boers, civilians, children and a German missionary died at their hands in the Northern Transvaal.

These were not cases of executions after verdicts had been handed down by a Military Court, but murder of persons laying down their arms and of prisoners of war. These scandalous killings were alleged to have taken place with the full knowledge of higher authority. The trial that followed throws considerable light on the attitude of the Military Courts regarding their meting out of justice during the war.

The Bushveld Carbineers consisted of volunteers and were formed during April 1901. Their objectives were clearly defined: to restrain all Boer guerilla bands in the North/Eastern Transvaal, to guard the railway line to the north from the Boers, to collect all Boer cattle and to eradicate anything that might be of assistance to the roving Boer commandos. The corps consisted mainly of Australians whose service time had expired. In its ranks were also to be found various colonials and Boer 'joiners', who had taken up arms against their own brethren for self-gain. It was a rough and undisciplined group of adventurers, whose officers were promoted overnight with little military experience. From their headquarters at Fort Edward, 90 kilometres north of Pietersburg, they launched their operations under the command of a Captain Taylor. He was a well-known, merciless sadist who fitted perfectly into Kitchener's plans to end the war as soon as possible by any means at their disposal.

The war in the Spelonke region to the north of Pietersburg soon deteriorated into a cruel confrontation with out-of-hand executions being standard procedure. This act was highlighted by the officers at their trial in which they stated that they had received specific orders from headquarters that, 'no prisoners are to be brought in'. Although some prisoners had been executed before, the spark hit the powder keg when Breaker Morant found the mutilated body of his bosom friend, Captain Hunt, during one of their sorties into the bush.

It later appeared that this was possibly the work of a witchdoctor. Morant accused the Boers and went beserk. What followed was a trail of revenge and murder. In the following six weeks, 23 people had died, including women and children and the German missionary Carl August Daniel Heese. It was actually the death of Heese that exposed these atrocities to the outside world. England feared a possible German protest and immediately ordered a full enquiry into the functions of the Carbineers. The following murders are documented, but it must be assumed that there were many more committed by the British military during this period.

Gerhard C Kooijker was bayoneted to death by British troops after surrendering. During the occupation of Pietersburg by the British, Kooijker shot and killed two British soldiers in a skirmish. When his hideout was discovered, he raised his hands in the air and shouted, 'I surrender'! He lies buried in the Pietersburg cemetery.

Six Boers rode in under a white flag to surrender on 2 July 1901. The British commanding officer, Captain Alfred Taylor, had ordered that no prisoners would be taken, and they were all shot immediately. Among them was the elderly JJ Geiser, who was suffering from fever and could not dismount from his cart. He was shot through the head in his cart. Taylor and his men were later found not guilty of murder. The six Boers lie buried on the farm Morgenson. The tombstone details the names as follows:

JF Vercuul	(31)
FGJ Potgieter	(18)
JJ Geiser	(65)
PJ Geiser	(11) (Possibly his grandson)
JC Greeling	(25)
Van Heerden	

Van Buuren was a 'joiner' who was shot and killed by Handcock on 4 July 1901 for pointing out who was responsible for the death of the six Boers to their widows.

Visser was wounded in a clash with the Australians on 11 August 1901. According to Morant, Visser was wearing the clothes of his murdered friend, Captain Hunt. Visser was dumped on a river bank near Duiwelskloof because he could not stand due to his wounds. He was shot and his grave is unknown.

Van den Berg was shot and killed during September 1901 on his farm Paardekraal behind Hangklip near Louis Trichardt in the presence of his wife and children. He was buried on the farm.

Eight Boers who had previously handed themselves over to British intelligence were sent to Morant and Taylor on 22 August 1901. They were paraded along the road and gunned down in cold blood. Only Morant was to be found guilty of this crime. One of the corps members who helped with the killings was a 'joiner', Theunis Botha.

The eight Boers are buried on the farm Ballymore in the Louis Trichardt district.

The remains of this weathered grave can still be found.

Their names are:

Baauwkens

Vahrmeyer WD

Smit CPJ

Logenaar

Westerhof GK

Wouters B

Du Preez JJ (16)

Pauskie

Reverend Carl August Daniel Heese was a German missionary who was shot to death on 23 August 1901 because he had witnessed the killings of the eight Boers the day before. A young black boy who was with Reverend Heese was shown no mercy and also shot, leaving no witnesses to the massacre. Although Morant and Handcock were found not guilty on this charge it was later discovered that a false alibi had been given. Handcock had in fact shot Heese and the boy on orders from Morant. Heese was buried where he fell but the youngster's grave is unknown. Heese was later reburied at the mission station at Makapaanspoort near Potgietersrus.

Two children were killed and one wounded on 5 September 1901 when a fusillade poured into their family's wagon while they were on the way to hand themselves over. The family had sent a message to the mission station that they were on their way. The screaming of the women did not deter the assassins and Jan Derk Grobler, aged 13, and young Daniel Grobler lay dead while their little sister was wounded in the neck.

Three Boers who were on their way to surrender at Fort Edward were shot down by Morant and his comrades on 7 September 1901. They were R van Staden and his two sons, C van Staden (17) and his youngest son, R van Staden (11). They lie buried together on the farm Sweetwaters near Ballymore in the Louis Trichardt district.

The 'joiner' Theunis Botha was also present at these killings. During the trial of Morant, Handcock and others, Botha was shot off his horse in front of the Pretoria prison and killed by an unknown assassin. This was clearly a case of revenge.

After the court of enquiry completed its investigations regarding these killings by the Bushveld Carbineers, a Military Court was established and sat behind closed doors in Pietersburg on 16 January 1902. On 26 February, the findings of the Military Court were made known. The two Australians, Morant and Handcock, had received the death sentence. The execution was carried out the following day in the courtyard of the Pretoria prison. They were buried in a communal grave in the cemetery. Another Australian, Witton, also received the death sentence, but it was committed to life imprisonment by Kitchener. Picton, an Englishman, received a dishonourable discharge from the forces. Three more British troops, Taylor, Robertson and Morrison, who were charged with the murder of various Boers, were released.

Morant, in his defence, testified that he had merely carried out the orders of his immediate superior, Captain Hunt, who in turn had received orders from Colonel Hamilton, the military secretary of Lord Kitchener. The order was short and emphatic: 'No prisoners to be brought in!' They had therefore interpreted this to mean that all prisoners were to be eliminated. When the Military Court held a special sitting in Pretoria to hear Hamilton's explanation, the fate of Morant and Handcock was sealed.

When asked if he had ever issued such an order on behalf of Kitchener, a very uncertain and nervous Colonel Hamilton answered with a short, 'No'. As a result of this answer, Morant and Handcock were sentenced to die.

When the news broke that the only two members of the Bushveld Carbineers who were to be executed were Australians, and that the English, including Taylor, were to get off scot-free, there was a passionate outcry from the Australian camp, who openly accused the court of being one-sided in that, firstly, the secrecy in which the Military Court conducted its business was contrary to the prescribed rules and regulations, as all Military Court hearings had to be held in public and open to the press. Secondly, that there was ample evidence against English officers who had murdered unarmed Boers and that no action was taken against them. Thirdly, that there was never a complete and official statement made by the British authorities regarding their findings. Historians during this period were advised that all the official documents had been destroyed. This, however, was not an isolated case of a possible cover-up. Many of the Military Court records simply disappeared and the doings of these hearings were swept under the proverbial carpet, where it was hoped they would remain, hidden forever.

The only information regarding the findings and performance of the Military Court is to be found in the book by Mitton, the Australian who was condemned to death but reprieved by Kitchener. After serving two years in a British prison, he was released and returned to Australia. In 1907 his book *Scapegoats of the Empire: The story of the Bushveldt Carbineers* was published in Australia.

In this book, he told the story of the Carbineers and referred to Kitchener as the Jewish priest who kicked the Australians into the desert. The Australian historians were now alerted to the fact that the trial was secret, unjust and covered up by the authorities, including Kitchener. The Australian government requested an explanation from His Lordship and received a rather unsatisfactory answer filled with untruths and distortions of the facts. This reply agitated the Australians to such an extent that they published his correspondence in the press.

The Australian Government felt so strongly about this case that it became a stipulated condition that none of their troops would be tried by a British Military Court during the 1914–1918 War. To many Australians, Morant and Handcock became national heroes and martyrs, and they were so depicted in the film *Breaker Morant*, released in 1980.

When reading this saga about the justice meted out by the British Military Courts during the Anglo-Boer War, a person can understand the lament of Gideon Scheepers after he had received his death sentence: 'Is it possible for me to be tried before such an unjust Court?'[14]

Conclusion

The Hague Convention

No war can be carried out in a civilised manner. War is always waged to kill your opponent by any possible means at your disposal. It is, therefore, always barbaric.

During the Hague Convention, which was attended by the leading civilised countries, a set of rules and guidelines was agreed upon. England subscribed to these, but the Republics did not sign the articles because they were not in attendance. They did, however, make known that they would abide by the outcome and thus the terms of the Convention were to govern the Anglo-Boer War.

At the outset of this conflict, a tacit silence prevailed regarding the participation of coloured people, colonials and civilians. Proclamations were originally issued to enable those in conflict to abide by certain agreements. However, as the war progressed and its nature changed, less notice was taken of the rules set down for conventional warfare.

With the eventual appearance of the concentration camps and the scorched-earth policies of the occupying forces, a total onslaught against civilians came into being. Britain, therefore, violated the Hague Convention and her deeds were contrary to the norms of civilised warfare. It can, therefore, be asked: By how much did the executions of condemned fighters violate this treaty?

High treason is a wilful crime. All rebels who took up arms against the Empire were thus guilty because they were legally British citizens. England did not acknowledge them as freedom fighters or soldiers at war. Under these conditions they were thus not allowed the status of prisoner of war according to international law, and any one of them could have been hanged. The execution of rebels was therefore not against the Convention's rules, but their selective execution was systematically conceived to discourage and frighten the population of the Cape Colony. These deeds were heavily criticised by British academics and interested overseas parties. The British press was emphatic that there were no grounds for executions unless all those found guilty of treason should receive the death penalty. Internment and banishment would have been more just and appropriate punishments, and would have engendered much less suffering and bitterness within Afrikaner circles.

The breaking of the oath of neutrality as well as the violation of parole agreements were also deeds of high treason. Cornelis Broeksma, with all his legal background, pleaded guilty to this charge in spite of the moral circumstances that surrounded his. Executions based on high treason were thus not deemed to be part of the Convention terms.

Murder and executions of prisoners and the wounded were all wilful acts, as were the continuation of conflict after surrender under the white flag, as well as espionage and treason. However false the reasons were for the trials and subsequent sentences imposed upon the population, they were not in violation of the Convention. But the executions of ordinary civilians, such as Hendrik van Heerden, flouted all the agreements regarding civilised warfare. He was wounded and a captive. The same applied to Pieter van Heerden, who was incapable of taking up arms because of his weight and poor eyesight.

Britain was also the transgressor of the rules in the case of Commandant Gideon Scheepers, who was executed for his treatment of spies and traitors. This was accepted practice according to the Convention, as was the destruction of railway equipment and lines of communication. And yet Boers like Scheepers and Breed paid the ultimate penalty because the British authorities classed these deeds as war crimes!

The burning and sacking of homes and the destruction of property and livestock of civilians were contraventions of the Hague Convention's terms. England once again changed the rules as her wrath descended upon helpless civilians. In retaliation, the commandos burned down homes and pillaged stock and provisions belonging to British sympathisers. England and not the Boers stands condemned before the world for their total disregard of the Hague Convention.

The most controversial issue of the war was the executions of black and coloured soldiers by the Boers when they were captured under arms. Although the participation of other races in the war was not a violation of the Convention, the Boers stated very clearly that they did not regard them as soldiers in a white man's war. Britain was also a party to this idea at the outbreak of hostilities, yet now the position was that England did not recognise the rebels as soldiers and they had to accept this fact. Both parties now took it upon themselves to execute any captured non-combatants. Proof of this is that although Commandant Conroy had 71 charges against him for the murder of coloured men under arms, he was not brought to trial after the war. In spite of this, some Republican burgers were executed for 'murder and attempted murder' of coloured soldiers. Again England violated the rules of fair and honest justice.

'Repulsive behaviour of a cruel and barbaric nature' and 'pillaging' were other charges brought against some of the executed. A case where a postmistress had her raincoat torn while wrestling for keys was enough for such charges to be formulated against the accused, who was executed. The major case of 'repulsive behaviour of a cruel and barbaric nature' must surely be the introduction of concentration camps and the scorched-earth policy. Again, the transgressor of human rights was both judge and executioner.

The injustice and unreasonable measures used by the British to secure prosecution and convictions against the Boers made a mockery of their judicial system. Again, these executions were not considered to be in contravention of the Hague Convention. What actually was a transgression of law and order was the fact that the victor was not to be challenged in court to defend accusations levelled against it.

The public executions, the compulsory attendance of the populace at these awful rituals, the summary disposal of the corpses, all went against the norms of civilised conflict. It was an abomination in the eyes of the world, and described by historians as unique in the history of civilised nations.

Eight years after these tragic episodes in the history of the Republics and Britain, the Union of South Africa came into being, largely due to attitudes of forgiveness and reconciliation. The dignified old Reverend AF Louw, brother of the executed Willie Louw, stated in his later years that he had asked the Lord for a small extension of the time for forgiveness.

Somewhere in the veld there is a small heap of stones.

Appendix A

Detailed below are names of rebels listed in the Military Blue Book at the National Archives in Cape Town (Files AG 3549, AG 3560). Note that the numbers begin at 17 and, in two instances, names have not been filled in.

ACT 6 OF 1900

17	HJ van Heerden	Sewefontein, Middelburg
18	CGJ Nienaber	De Bad, Hanover
19	JP Nienaber	De Bad, Hanover
20	JA Nieuwoudt	De Bad, Hanover
21	AC Jooste	Boven Narries, Kenhardt
22	PW Klopper	Kleinfontein, Albert
23	HL Jacobs	Labour Colony, Kenhardt
24	FA Marais	Langkloof, Middelburg
25	CJ Claassen	Bouwersfontein, Somerset East
26	JP Coetzee	Paardekraal, Cradock
27	LFS Pfeiffer	Leeuwfontein, Victoria West
28	PJ Fourie	Uitkomst, Jansenville
29	JBL van Rensburg	Aberdeen
30	HJ Veenstra	Rietfontein, Murraysburg
31	F Toe	Gottenburg, Sweden
32	IW Nel	Bulkraal, Graaff-Reinet
33	DF Olwagen	Graaff-Reinet
34	H van Vuuren	Hottentotsrivier, Willowmore
35	JH Roux	Jordaanskraal, Albany
36	JGW Jansen	New York, Vryburg
37	NC Rautenbach	Massoukop, Vryburg
38	JG Schoeman	Groot Zeekoegat, Tarkastad
39	JC Lötter	Naauwpoort
40	PJ Wolfaardt	Fair View, Middelburg
41		
42	J Kuhn	Zoetlief, Vryburg
43	H Kuhn	Zoetlief, Vryburg
44	PW van Heerden	Vaalvlei, Tarkastad
45	NF van Wyk	Mountain World, Victoria West
46		
47	WH Louw	Achtertang, Colesberg

All the above were executed.

Appendix B

Extracts from Military Court Records in the Cape Colony Regarding Trials

Spellings and details as per charge sheets found in the Cape Archives. Ref: AG 3534, AG 3635, AG 3636, AG 3560. Military Blue Book.

HENDRIK JACOBUS VAN HEERDEN. Farmer/Shopkeeper.
From the farm Zewefontein, near Spitzkop under the Doornberg, Middelburg District. Tried *in absentia* by a Military Court formed by Lt Col CF Gorringe at the adjoining farm, Riet valley, on 2/3/1901.

Capt CE Wilson	East Lancashire Regiment	President
Capt A Bailey	CDF	
Capt collet	CDF	
Lt Geard	CDF	

Lt Kirby severely wounded and others had slight wounds. Van heerden was executed by firing squad shortly after the Military Court had reached its decision.

STATEMENT BY LT COL GORRINGE
After the above Court had been held and the column I command were on march towards Pearston I received by rider Lt Kirby's report. He was so badly wounded he could not attend. This report strictly confirmed Van Heerden's guilt and treachery and I caused it necessary to make a summary example on the spot. I could not wait for confirmation from higher authority as it was imperative that the enemy, then on the march to Pearston, should be followed up without delay. I therefore confirmed the sentence which I ordered to be carried out. I detached a squadron for that purpose.
GF Gorringe
Lt Col

CONFIRMATION OF SENTENCE
I hereby confirm the finding and sentence of death in the case of Van Heerden and in the case of the above sentence of death. I am of the opinion that by reason of the exigencies of active service and the urgent necessity for an example on the spot, it is not practical, having due regard for the public service, to delay the case for confirmation by any qualified officer superior to myself. Signed this 2nd day of March 1901.
GF Gorringe Lt Col
Gen Field Officer in Chief Command of forces operating in the vicinity of Riet Valley.

Capt Smolle of F Squadron arrived at Zewefontein and kicked the door open of the bedroom where Van Heerden was lying nursed by his wife and Mr Mamby, a teacher on the farm school, and his book keeper.

CONFIRMATION OF EXECUTION

The promulgation and sentence of death of Hendrik Jacobus van Heerden was carried out on 2nd March 1901.

FW Lawrence Wickstead

Lt F Squad. Col Gorringe's

Flying column

This act of execution was later approved by Lord Kitchener and placed on record under the section of Cape Rebels.

The above act by the Military Court was brought to the notice of the Colonial Parliament in Cape Town, the extract is as follows:

HJ VAN HEERDEN. Minute 1/31 of 27th April.

CABINET: Subject. Shooting of Hendrik Jacobus van Heerden at Zevenfontein by the Imperial Military Authorities. [This was a circular for the attention of the Cabinet, who had to initial it after reading the details]

The Hon Prime Minister	
The Hon Colonial Secretary	Initialed by him 15/5
The Hon The Treasurer	
The Hon The Attorney-General	
The Hon The Commissioner of Public Works	Initialed
The Hon The Secretary for Agriculture	Initialed 23/5

PRIME MINISTER'S OFFICE

15/5/1901

Lord Kitchener's letter dated in Pretoria from Army Headquarters on 7/5/1901 addressed as follows:

SGC NIENABER, JP NIENABER, JA NIEUWOUDT

Tried at De Aar on 5/3/1901. Lt Gen the Hon H Lyttleton formed a Military Court consisting of:

Lt Col AE Codrington	Coldstream Guards	President
Maj HS Horne	RHA	
Capt HF Warden	The Queens RWSR	
Capt CE Morgan	Colonial Forces	
Lt R Peel	Colonial Forces	
Capt WJL McDonald		Prosecutor
FE Konig		Interpreter
G Gradwell		Interpreter

Executed by firing squad at De Aar on 19/3/1901

AC JOOSTE, HL JACOBS
Tried at Kenhardt on 3/6/1901 and 7/6/1901. Lt Col Cann, Police Commissioner Kimberley formed a Military Court consisting of:

Capt JT White	Cape Police, OC Troops, Kenhardt	President
Lt WM Eustace	Acting Cmdt, Kenhardt	
Lt ON McLeod	OC Settles Scouts	
Lt CH West	Cmdt, Town Guards, Kenhardt	Prosecutor
GG van Breda	Clerk of Court for Regional magistrate	Interpreter
Mr M Sachs	Attorney, Kenhardt	Defence

Executed by firing squad at Kenhardt on 24/7/1901.

PW KLOPPER
Tried at Steynsburg on 17/6/1901. Military Court consisted of:

Lt Col W Doran	Royal Irish Rifles President	
Maj RL Mullins	Brabants Horse	
Lt TP Dawson	PAGMI	
PJ vd Poe		Interpreter

Executed by hanging at Burgersdorp on 20/7/1901.

FA MARAIS, JP COETZEE, CJ CLAASSEN
Tried at Dordrecht on 24/6/1901. Military Court consisted of:

Lt Col W Doran	Royal Irish Rifles	President
Maj RL Mullins	Brabants Horse	
Lt. TP Dawson	PAGMI	
Capt CG Huddlestone		Prosecutor
Mr WD van Alphen		Interpreter

FA Marais executed by hanging at Middelburg on 10/7/1901.
JP Coetzee executed by hanging at Cradock on 13/7/1901.
CJ Claassen executed by hanging at Somerset East on 24/7/1901.

PJ FOURIE, JBL VAN RENSBURG, LFS PFEIFFER
Tried at Graaff-Reinet on 30/7/1901. Military Court consisted of:

Lt Col W Doran	Royal Irish Rifles	President
Maj RL Mullins	Brabants Horse	
Lt TP Dawson	PAGMI	
Capt Sandys Lumsdaine	HLI	Prosecutor
Sgt Peters	Police	Interpreter

Executed by firing squad at Graaff-Reinet on 19/8/1901.

DF OLWAGEN, IW NEL.
Tried at Graaff-Reinet on 2/8/1901. Military Court consisted of:

Lt Col W Doran	Royal Irish Rifles	President

Maj RL Mullins	Brabants Horse	
Lt TP Dawson	PAGMI	
Capt Sandys Lumsdaine	HLI	Prosecutor
JP Burger		Interpreter

Executed by firing squad at Graaff-Reinet on 26/8/1901.

H van VUUREN, F TOE, HJ VEENSTRA

Tried at Graaff-Reinet on 2/8/1901, 5/8/1901, 5/8/1901. Military Court consisted of:

Lt Col W Doran	Royal Irish Rifles	President
Maj RL Mullins	Brabants Horse	
Lt TP Dawson	PAGMI	
Capt Sandys Lumsdaine	HLI	Prosecutor
Mr Palmer		Interpreter

Executed by firing squad at Colesberg on 4/9/1901.

JH ROUX

Tried at Graaff-Reinet on 30/8/1901. Military Court consisted of:

Lt Col W Doran	Royal Irish Rifles	President
Maj RL Mullins	Brabants Horse	
Lt TP Dawson	PAGMI	
Capt Sandys Lumsdaine	HLI	Prosecutor
Sgt Peters	Police	Interpreter
Mr Thomas Auret	Attorney	Defence

Executed by firing squad at Graaff-Reinet on 7/10/1901.

JGW HANSEN, NC RAUTENBACH

Tried at Vryburg on 10/9/1901. Lt Col WH Murray formed a Military Court consisting of:

Lt Col AT Perkins	3rd Welsh Regiment	President
Capt H Lake	RFA	
Capt FP Latham	3rd Welsh Regiment	

Executed by hanging at Vryburg on 11/10/1901.

JG SCHOEMAN

Tried at Graaff-Reinet on 17/9/1901. Military Court consisted of:

Lt Col W Doran	Royal Irish Rifles	President
Maj RL Mullins	Brabants Horse	
Lt TP Dawson	PAGMI	
Capt Sandys Lumsdaine	HLI	Prosecutor
Sgt Peters	Police	Interpreter

Executed by firing squad at Tarkastad on 12/10/1901.

PF WOLFAARDT, W KRUGER

Tried at Graaff-Reinet on 26/9/1901. Lt Gen Sir JDP French KCB ordered a Military Court consisting of:

Lt Col W Doran	Royal Irish Rifles	President
Maj RL Mullens (sic)	Brabants Horse	
Lt TP Dawson	PAGMI	
Capt FM Sandys Lumsdaine	2nd HLI	Prosecutor
Sgt Peters	Police	Interpreter
Mr T Auret	Attorney	Defence

PJ Wolfaardt executed by firing squad at Middelburg on 15/10/1901.
W Kruger executed by firing squad at Cradock on 17/10/1901.

DC BREED No records at Cape Archives.

CMDT JC LÖTTER

Tried at Graaff-Reinet on 27/9/1901. Lt Gen Sir JDP French KCB ordered a Military Court consisting of:

Lt Col W Doran	Royal Irish Rifles	President
Maj RL Mullins	Brabants Horse	
Lt TP Dawson	PAGMI	
Capt Sandys Lumsdaine	2nd HLI	Prosecutor
Sgt Peters	Police	Interpreter

Executed by firing squad at Middelburg on 12/10/1901.

H KUHN, J KUHN

Tried at Vryburg on 30/9/1901. No records of Military Court available.
Executed by hanging at Vryburg on 29/10/1901.

NF VAN NIEKERK

Tried at Graaff-Reinet on 2/10/1901. Military Court consisted of:

Lt Col W Doran	Royal Irish Rifles	President
Maj RL Mullens (sic)	Brabants Horse	
Lt TP Dawson	PAGMI	
Capt FM Sandys Lumsdaine	2nd HLI	Prosecutor
Sgt Peters	Police	Interpreter

Executed by firing squad at Colesberg on 12/11/1901.

PW VAN HEERDEN. Farmer.

Tried at Graaff-Reinet on 10/10/1901. Military Court consisted of:

Lt Col W Doran	Royal Irish Rifles	President
Maj RL Mullens (sic)	Brabants Horse	
Lt TP Dawson	PAGMI	

| Capt Sandys Lumsdaine | HLI | Prosecutor |
| Sgt Peters | Police | Interpreter |

Executed by firing squad at Tarkastad on 12/11/1901.

WH LOUW

Tried at Graaff-Reinet on 4/11/1901. Military Court consisted of:

Lt Col W Doran	Royal Irish Rifles	President
Maj RL Mullins	Brabants Horse	
Lt TP Dawson	PAGMI	
Capt Sandys Lumsdaine	HLI	Prosecutor
Sgt Peters	Police	Interpreter

Executed by firing squad at Colesberg on 23/11/1901.

IB LIEBENBERG

Tried at Aliwal North on 22/11/1901. Military Court consisted of:

Col Hughes-Hallet	Seaforth Highlanders	President
Maj Garland	HLI	
Capt Earle	3rd Lancashire Regiment	
Capt CP Halse		Prosecutor
Alleyne Yeld		Interpreter

Executed by hanging at Aliwal North on 11/1/1902.

CMDT GJ SCHEEPERS

Tried at Graaff-Reinet on 18/12/1901. Military Court consisted of:

Lt Col P Sprot	The Carbineers	President
Capt CE Wilson	Lancashire Fusileers	
Lt TP Dawson	PAGMI	
Capt EC Tennant	Intelligence Officer	Prosecutor
Mr T Auret		Defence

Executed by firing squad at Graaff-Reinet on 18/1/1902.

JF GELDENHUYS

Tried at Graaff-Reinet on 18/1/1902. Military Court consisted of:

Lt Col A Sprat (sic)	The Carbineers	President
Capt HA Chandos Pole-Gell	Coldstream Guards	
Lt TP Dawson	PAGMI	
Capt Sandys Lumsdain (sic)	HLI	Prosecutor
Sgt Peters	Police	Interpreter

Executed by firing squad at Graaff-Reinet on 14/2/1902.

FE DU RANDT

Tried at Cradock on 7/3/1902. Military Court consisted of:

Lt Col GFH St. John	Royal Artillery	President
Capt H Chandos Pole-Gel	Coldstream Guards	
Lt TP Dawson	PAGMI	
Capt FM Sandys Lumsdain (sic)	HLI	Prosecutor
Mr PG Martin		Interpreter

Executed by firing squad at Cradock on 5/4/1902.

P DE RUYT. No trial records. Shot after capture near Glen Lynden, Bedford.

CL VERMAAS. No trial records. Shot after capture near Kariega Siding.

H RITTENBERG. No trial records. Shot after capture near Kariega Siding.

A VAN ONSELEN. No trial records. Shot after capture near Kariega Siding.

JA BAXTER. No trial records. Shot after capture at Goewermentsvlei, Aberdeen.

P BESTER. No trial records. Shot after capture at Marsh Hill, Dordrecht.

FE DAVIS. No trial records. Shot at Somerset East.

A RENIKE. No trial records. Hanged at Mafeking.

L BRINK. No trial records. Hanged at Mafeking.

H KUHN. No trial records. Hanged at Vryburg.

J KUHN. No trial records. Hanged at Vryburg.

DC BREED. No trial records. Shot at Cradock.

Cape Archives. AG 3634, AG 3635, AG 3636. Note the different spellings of certain names on the charge sheets and court records.

APPENDIX C

Statistics of Trials and Executions

SECTION I – CAPE COLONY

Citizenship of the executed

Cape rebels. Known and confirmed	30
Burgers who claimed they were Republican citizens, but were executed as rebels	2
Foreigners executed as rebels	2
Transvalers	6
Free Staters (One was executed as a rebel)	2
Deserters from the British Police or Army	2
TOTAL	**44**

Ages of the executed

16–20 years old	5
21–30 years old	24
31–40 years old	9
41–50 years old	5
51 and over	1
TOTAL	**44**

Places of execution

Graaff-Reinet	8
Colesberg	5
Cradock	4
Vryburg	4
Middelburg	3
Middelburg District, Sewefontein	1
Tarkastad	2
Uitenhage District, Zuurberge Region	3
Somerset East	2
Mafeking	2
Kenhardt	2
Dordrecht District, Marsh Hill	1
Aliwal North	1
Aberdeen District, Goewermentsvlei	1
Burgersdorp	1
Bedford District, Glen Lynden	1
De Aar	3
TOTAL	**44**

Method of execution

Hanged	11
Firing Squad	29
Died by firing squad without trial	
Caught wearing khaki uniforms allegedly taken from British troops	4
TOTAL	**44**

Rebel Sentences

Total under arms, punished and disenfranchised	10,577
Condemned to death and executed. (This does not include seven burgers from the Transvaal and Free State)	35
Condemned to death but reprieved	335
Banned to Bermuda as convicts with hard labour	360
Prison sentences served	1,012

Type of charges taken from the charge sheets of the executed

High treason, active in arms	32
Murder of British soldiers	10
Murder of coloured persons	13
Attempted murder of British soldiers	18
Attempted murder of coloured persons	2
Arson	20
Plunder and theft of horses, donkeys and provisions	12
Captured in khaki uniforms	5
In possession of soft-nose bullets	4
Wrecking railway lines and derailment of trains	3
Deserters from the British forces	2
Giving aid to the Boer forces	1
Treachery	1

Commemorated	The 44 executed

Graves, known and identified	27
Unknown graves	17
TOTAL	**44**

Photographs available 32
None available 12
TOTAL 44

Mentioned on graves and monuments 38
Nowhere mentioned in three towns 6
TOTAL 44

The above statistics are based on figures obtained from Government Blue Books, Snyman: *Rebelleverhore*, Scheepers-Strydom: *Kaapland in die Tweede Vryheidsoorlog*, Constantine: *The Guerilla War in the Cape Colony*.

SECTION 2 – TRANSVAAL AND FREE STATE

Tried by Military Courts and executed
Free State 5
Transvaal 16
Natal (Uncertain, 1 or 2) 1
TOTAL 22

Executions without trial
Transvaal (only documented cases) 24

Methods of execution
Hanged 2
Died by firing squad 44
TOTAL 46

Types of charges taken from the charge sheets of the executed
Murder and attempted murder 5
Fired under the white flag 5
Violation of the oath of neutrality and parole 5
Captured wearing khaki clothes 4
Conspiracy and high treason 3
Poisoning of horses
In possession of firearms 2
Spying 1
Shooting a wounded prisoner 1
Inciting persons to take up arms against Her Majesty's forces 1
Deserting and joining the Boer force 1
Detonating and wrecking a train 1

Statistics obtained from the sources in Section 2.

229

APPENDIX D

Sources

SECTION 1:
EXECUTIONS IN THE CAPE COLONY

CHAPTER 1
(1) Statistics in Appendix C
(2) See Hendrik Schoeman in Chapter 10

CHAPTER 2
(1) Venter: *Ons Geskiedenisalbum*, p.617.
(2) Botha: *Graaff-Reinet tydens die Anglo-Boereoorlog*, p.133-134.
(3) Snyman: *Die Afrikaner in Kaapstad*, p.167.
(4) Breytenbach: *Gedenkalbum*, p.471: Snyman: *Afrikaner in Kaapland*, p.167.
(5) Constantine: *Guerilla War in the Cape Colony*, pp.3-5.
(6) Witnesses in the trials of Wolfaardt, Kruger, Breedt, Klopper and others.
(7) Witnesses of Willie Louw at his trial, Chapter 12. Botha: *Graaff-Reinet tydens die Anglo-Boereoorlog*, p.138.
(8) Snyman: *Rebelleverhore*, p.69-70.
(9) Snyman: *Rebelleverhore*, p.61, re. Execution of Petrus Coetzee.
(10) Terminology used on the charge sheets of the condemned.
(11) Snyman: *Rebelleverhore*, p.62.
(12) Spies: *Methods of Barbarism*, p.35.
(13) Snyman: *Rebelleverhore*, p.70.
(14) From: *Gebed om die Gebeente*, DJ Opperman.
(15) JF Preller in *Gedenkalbum van die Tweede Vryheidsoorlog* from Breytenbach, p.396.

CHAPTER 3
(1) Snyman: *Rebelleverhore*, p.46-47.
(2) Botha: *Graaff-Reinet tydens die Anglo-Boereoorlog*, p.143.
(3) Snyman: *Rebelleverhore*, pp.62, 68: Breytenbach: *Gedenkalbum*, pp.487-488: Botha: *Graaff-Reinet Tydens die Anglo-Boereoorlog*, p.120.

(4) Terminology and examples regarding cases discussed in the book.
(5) Executions of Fourie, Van Rensburg, Pfeiffer and Scheepers.
(6) Execution of Cornelius Claassen in Somerset East.
(7) Extract from *Cape Times*, (Snyman p.49).
(8) *Northern Post*, 17 July 1901.

CHAPTER 4
(1) Compiled from Breytenbach: *Gedenkalbum*, pp.492-495. Snyman: *Rebelleverhore*, pp.54-55: Jordaan: *Hoe Zij Stierven*.
(2) Blue Book in Cape Archives: Trial of Hendrik van Heerden.
(3) Snyman: *Rebelleverhore*, p.34.
(4) Ibid p.35.
(5) Ibid p.36.
(6) According to Jordaan, *Hoe Zij Stierven*; Snyman: *Rebelleverhore* pp.36-38.
(7) Constantine: *The Guerilla War in the Cape Colony*, p.36.

CHAPTER 5
(1) Historical background in Oosthuizen: *Rebelle van Stormberge*, pp.150-152.
(2) Snyman: *Rebelleverhore*, pp.148-151, Pakenham: *The Boer War*, p.514; Shearing: *The Second Invasion of the Cape Colony* p.174.
(3) Report in *Somerset East Budget*, 25 July 1901 and in Jordaan: *Hoe Zij Stierven*.
(4) Breytenbach: *Gedenkalbum*, p.471.
(5) According to: Snyman: *Rebelleverhore*, Jordaan: *Hoe Zij Stierven*, Oosthuizen: *Rebelle van die Stormsberge*.
(6) Snyman: *Rebelleverhore*, p.61.
(7) Ibid p.58.
(8) Events according to: Jordaan, *Hoe Zij Stierven*, Snyman: *Rebelleverhore* pp.56-59.
(9) *Somerset East Budget*, 10 July 1901.

CHAPTER 6

(1) Oosthuizen: *Rebelle van die Stormberge*, p.34.
(2) Events according to: Jordaan: *Hoe Zij Stierven;* Snyman, *Rebelleverhore* pp.50–51, *Gedenkalbum* pp.504-506.
(3) *Brandwag:* 4 June 1948.
(4) *Brandwag:* 4 June 1948.
(5) Snyman: *Rebelleverhore*, p.58; Shearing: *The Second Invasion of the Cape Colony*, p.75.
(6) Snyman: *Rebelleverhore*, pp.59-60.
(7) Spies: *Methods of Barbarism*, p.240.
(8) Breytenbach: *Gedenkalbum*, p.496.

CHAPTER 7

(1) Statistics from Botha: *Graaff-Reinet tydens die Anglo-Boereoorlog* pp.85, 146.
(2) Extract from the diary of Lt.Col. H Scobell.
(3) Figures from Rodney Constantine: *The Guerilla War in the Cape Colony*, p.84.
(4) Reports on Fourie, Van Rensburg and Pfeiffer according to: *Hoe Zij Stierven* and the Blue Book.
(5) Snyman: *Rebelleverhore*, p.61.
(6) According to *Hoe Zij Stierven*, p.65 and Botha: *Graaff-Reinet tydens die Anglo-Boereoorlog*, p.153.
(7) According to *Hoe Zij Stierven* and information from JC Loock: Ref. The diary of Major H Shute.
(8) Smith: *A History of the Graaff-Reinet district*, p.113; Botha: *Graaff-Reinet tydens die Anglo-Boereoorlog*, p.160; in cooperation with JC Loock.

CHAPTER 8

(1) Data from Government Blue Book.
(2) Details from *Hoe Zij Stierven*.
(3) Jordaan: *Hoe Zij Stierven*, pp.118, 161.
(4) Schalk du Toit: *Ontstaan van die Gemeente Nuwe Kerk op Graaff-Reinet/*
(5) Botha: *Graaff-Reinet tydens die Anglo-Boereoorlog*, p.8.
(6) Ibid p.224.
(7) Shearing: *The Second Invasion of the Cape Colony*, p.56; Spies: *Methods of Barbarism*. p.232.
(8) Botha: *Graaff-Reinet tydens the Anglo-Boereoorlog*, p.225.
(9) Spies: *Methods of Barbarism*, p.232; Botha: *Graaff-Reinet tydens die Anglo-Boereoorlog*, p.225.
(10) Botha: *Graaff-Reinet tydens die Anglo-Boereoorlog*, p.226.

CHAPTER 9

(1) Information from *Hoe Zij Stierven* and Blue Book.
(2) Ibid.
(3) Ibid.

CHAPTER 10

(1) Events according to the diary of Lt.-Col. H Scobell. Newspaper clippings from the *Graaff-Reinet Advertiser* in the Graaff-Reinet Museum; Shearing: *The Second Invasion of the Cape Colony*, pp.39, 134-135; Constantine: *The Guerilla War in the Cape Colony*, p.88; Breytenbach: *Gedenkalbum*, pp.499-500.
(2) Figures from Shearing: *The Second Invasion of the Cape Colony*, p.137. Constantine: *The Guerilla War in the Cape Colony*, p.88.
(3) Additional information from newspaper clippings regarding the hearings and sentences from the *Graaff-Reinet Advertiser* in the Museum; Snyman: *Rebelleverhore*, pp.53-54.
(4) Compiled from *Hoe Zij Stierven:* Newspaper clippings from the *Graaff-Reinet Advertiser* in the Museum; Breytenbach: *Gedenkalbum* pp.499-500.
(5) Breytenbach: *Gedenkalbum*, p.490.
(6) According to *Hoe Zij Stierven* and charge sheets in the Blue Book.
(7) Shearing: *The Second Invasion of the Cape Colony*, p.236.
(8) Trial record at Cape Archives and newspaper report from the *Graaff-Reinet Advertiser.*
(9) According to Jordaan: *Hoe Zij Stierven;* Constantine: *The Guerilla War in the Cape Colony*, p.52, article found in old gaol at Cradock.
(10) Article found in old gaol at Cradock; Jordaan: *Hoe Zij Stierven*.
(11) Newspaper clippings from *Graaff-*

Reinet Advertiser; Jordaan: *Hoe Zij Stierven* and Breytenbach: *Gedenkalbum* p.502.

CHAPTER 11
(1) Reitz: *Commando*, p.233.
(2) *Huisgenoot*, 17 January 1945; Reitz: *Commando*, pp.241-242. Constantine: *The Guerilla War in the Cape Colony*, p.89; Shearing: *The Second Invasion of the Cape Colony*, p.144.
(3) Shearing: *The Second Invasion of the Cape Colony*, p.144.
(4) *Huisgenoot*, 17 January 1945.
(5) Reitz: *Commando*, p.255; Jordaan: *Hoe Zij Stierven;* Shearing: *The Second Invasion of the Cape Colony*, pp.144-145.
(6) Cooperation with JC Loock.
(7) The diary of Lt.Col. H Scobell pp.64-65 in the possession of Dr Arnold van Dyk, Bloemfontein.
(8) Shearing: *The Second Invasion of the Cape Colony.* p.145; SB Spies and G Mattrass: Jan Smuts: *Memoirs of the Boer War.*
(9) Shearing: *The Second Invasion of the Cape Colony*, p.236; cooperation with JC Loock.

CHAPTER 12
(1) Breytenbach: *Gedenkalbum*, p.502.
(2) Van Zyl: *Helde-album*, p.321.
(3) Shearing: *The Second Invasion of the Cape Colony*, pp.176-177.
(4) Jordaan: *Hoe Zij Stierven.* p.41.
(5) Breytenbach: *Gedenkalbum*, pp.482-484; Shearing: *The Second Invasion of the Cape Colony*, p.176; Meintjies: *Stormberg*, p.142; Constantine: *The Guerilla War in the Cape Colony*, p.14.
(6) Van Zyl: *Helde-album*, p.321; Spies: *Methods of Barbarism*, p.206.
(7) Snyman: *Rebelleverhore*, p.63.
(8) According to Jordaan: *Hoe Zij Stierven;* Van Zyl: *Helde-album*, p.32. Breytenbach: *Gedenkalbum*, pp.500-502.
(9) Eugene van Heerden: *Philipstown 100 Jaar*, p.47.

CHAPTER 13
(1) Snyman: *Rebelleverhore*, pp.55, 62.

(2) According to Breytenbach: *Gedenkalbum*, pp.495-496; Snyman: *Rebelleverhore*, pp.54-55; Jordaan: *Hoe Zij Stierven;* Government Blue Book.
(3) Extract from Breytenbach: *Gedenkalbum*, p.496.
(4) According to Snyman: *Rebelleverhore*, pp.51-52; Jordaan: *Hoe Zij Stierven;* Newspaper clippings from *Graaff-Reinet Advertiser* in the Graaff-Reinet Museum.
(5) Snyman: *Rebelleverhore*, p.53.
(6) Jordaan: *Hoe Zij Stierven;* Newspaper clippings from the *Graaff-Reinet Advertiser* in the Graaff-Reinet Museum.
(7) Jordaan: *Hoe Zij Stierven;* Government Blue Book.

CHAPTER 14
(1) According to Dr Eben Greyling: *Tussen die Berge;* Constantine: *The Guerilla War in the Cape Colony*, pp.54, 57, 63; *Northern Post*, 27 November 1901; Du Plessis: *Oomblikke van Spanning*, pp.42, 61.
(2) Blue Book, *Witnesses in the trial of Willie Louw.*
(3) Wilson: *After Pretoria*, Vol V, p.752.
(4) According to the *Somerset East Budget*, 25 January 1902; Jordaan: *Hoe Zij Stierven;* Shearing: *The Second Invasion of the Cape Colony*, pp.211, 236.
(5) According to *Northern Post*, 22 November 1901, 7, 23 and 27 December 1901; Prinsloo: *Smithfield*, p.443; Jordaan: *Hoe Zij Stierven; Oorlogsherinneringe van Witkop von Caues* (Unpublished).
(6) Garden of Remembrance for the British fallen in Aliwal North.

CHAPTER 15
(1) Warwick: *Black People and the S.A. War*, p.6.
(2) Ibid pp.15, 16.
(3) Nasson: *Abraham Esau's War*, p.14.
(4) Warwick: *Black People and the S.A. War*, pp.22-24.
(5) Ibid pp.25, 26.

(6) Pretorius: *Kommandolewe*, p.288.

(7) Constantine: *The Guerilla War in the Cape Colony*, pp.36-38.

(8) Oosthuizen: *Rebelle van die Stormberge*, p.194.

(9) Warwick: *Black People and the S.A. War*, p.121; Pretorius: *Kommandolewe*, pp.291-292; Snyman: *Die Afrikaner in Kaapland*, p.104; Shearing: *The Second Invasion of the Cape Colony*, pp.102-103.

(10) Nasson: *Abraham Esau's War*, p.22.

(11) Pretorius: *Kommandolewe*, p.292.

(12) Warwick: *Black People and the S.A. War*, p.25.

(13) Constantine: *The Guerilla War in the Cape Colony*, p.149.

(14) Ibid p.163.

(15) Shearing: *The Second Invasion of the Cape Colony*, p.103.

(16) Pretorius: *Kommandolewe*, p.295; Shearing: *The Second Invasion of the Cape Colony*, p.198; Constantine: *The Guerilla War in the Cape Colony*, p.39.

CHAPTER 16

(1) Warwick: *Black People and the S.A. War*, p.121.

(2) Constantine: *The Guerilla War in the Cape Colony*, p.36.

(3) Ibid p.41.

(4) Roodt: *Die Kaapse Rebel*, pp.200, 220. NB. Conroy was not one of the three Boers who were refused amnesty at the peace conference and who had to stand trial for war crimes. See Chapter 2, Section 11, in *Christiaan de Wet Annale* No. 6, pp.51, 56.

(5) Article regarding the unveiling of the Burger Monument in Kenhardt for the Boer fallen during the Anglo-Boer War 1899–1902 as supplied by Mrs Martha Jooste of Kenhardt; Constantine: *The Guerilla War in the Cape Colony*, p.139; Roodt: *Die Rebel*, Chapters 8 and 9.

(6) Jordaan: *Hoe Zij Stierven*; Articles from Mrs Martha Jooste in Kenhardt.

CHAPTER 17

(1) Van Zyl: *Helde-album*, p.133.

(2) Shearing: *The Second Invasion of the Cape Colony*, p.232.

(3) Warwick: *Black People and the S.A. War*, pp.30-38.

(4) Constantine: *The Guerilla War in the Cape Colony*, pp.12, 14.

(5) Renike and Brink according to Jordaan: *Hoe Zij Stierven*; Shearing: *The Second Invasion of the Cape Colony*, pp.232, 235; Constantine: *The Guerilla War in the Cape Colony*, pp.12-14.

CHAPTER 18

(1) *Gedenkboek van Vryburg*; Constantine: *The Guerilla War in the Cape Colony*, pp.10-14.

(2) According to the *Gedenkboek van Vryburg*.

(3) According to Jordaan: *Hoe Zij Stierven*; *Gedenkboek van Vryburg*; Shearing: *The Second Invasion of the Cape Colony*, pp.233, 235; Constantine: *The Guerilla War in the Cape Colony*, pp.10-14.

(4) Ibid.

CHAPTER 19

(1) Breytenbach: *Gedenkalbum*, p.489.

(2) Shearing: *The Second Invasion of the Cape Colony* as ref. from *Trial of Scheepers* by Stanford.

(3) Breytenbach: *Gedenkalbum*, p.490.

(4) Shearing: *The Second Invasion of the Cape Colony*, p.238.

(5) Snyman: *Rebelleverhoor*, p.62, as reported in the *Morning Leader*.

(6) Shearing: *The Second Invasion of the Cape Colony*, pp.239, 241; *Rebelleverhoor*, p.65; Breytenbach: *Gedenkalbum*, p.491.

(7) Snyman: *Rebelleverhore*, pp.63-64.

(8) Breytenbach: *Gedenkalbum*, p.491.

(9) Testified in trial of JJ de Jager in Section 2.

(10) Warwick: *Black People in the S.A. War*, pp.18, 20, 26.

(11) Warwick: *Black People in the S.A. War*, p.121; Meintjies: *Stormberg*, pp.161-162; Botha: *Graaff-Reinet tydens die Anglo-Boereoorlog*, p.152.

(12) Breytenbach: *Gedenkalbum*, pp.489-490; Botha: *Graaff-Reinet tydens die Anglo-Boereoorlog*, p.149.

(13) Shearing: *The Second Invasion of the Cape Colony*, pp.239-242.

(14) Ibid p.194.

(15) Breytenbach: *Gedenkalbum*, p.474-475; Radioprogram, 'Wat sê die Reg' 18/8/1997 by Nicky vd Berg regarding the Smith trial.

(16) Van Zyl: *Helde-album*, pp.223, 383-385; cooperation Rodney Constantine.

(17) Snyman: *Rebelleverhore*, p.68.

(18) These telegrams have recently been acquired by the War Museum in Bloemfontein.

(19) Jordaan: *Hoe Zij Stierven*; Breytenbach: *Gedenkalbum*, pp.488-491.

(20) Constantine: *The Guerilla War in the Cape Colony*, p.163.

(21) Shearing: *The Second Invasion of the Cape Colony*, pp.131-133.

(22) Constantine: *The Guerilla War in the Cape Colony*, pp.158-159; Preller: *The Diary of Scheepers*, p.136. Printed articles quoted by Constantine.

(23) Diary of Lt.-Col. H Scobell in the possession of Dr Arnold van Dyk of Bloemfontein.

(24) Botha: *Graaff-Reinet tydens die Anglo-Boereoorlog*, p.153.

(25) Information regarding the grave of Scheepers received from Johan Loock in Bloemfontein; Botha: *Graaff-Reinet tydens die Anglo-Boereoorlog*, pp.158, 160.

(26) From *Gebed om die gebeente* by DJ Opperman. These words appear on the small stone monument erected in memory of Gideon Scheepers, near his place of execution outside Graaff-Reinet on the road to Murraysburg.

CHAPTER 20

(1) Breytenbach: *Gedenkalbum*, pp.183-184.

(2) Snyman: *Rebelleverhore*, p.61.

(3) According to Jordaan in *Hoe Zij Stierven*; Articles found in the old gaol at Cradock; Government Blue Book.

(4) Du Randt refers to Rev. Murray as Doctor. Rev. Murray was not a doctor, although he studied as a medical missionary in Scotland. He then became a medical missionary in Nyasaland and was occasionally addressed as Doctor. He was a regular visitor to the interned prisoners at the old Graaff-Reinet prison. (Information supplied by Dr Schalk du Toit of Murraysburg.)

SECTION 2
EXECUTIONS IN THE TRANSVAAL AND FREE STATE

INTRODUCTION

(1) *Christiaan de Wet Annale*, No. 6, pp.61-62.

(2) Conan Doyle: *The War in South Africa*, pp.129-130.

(3) Spies: *Methods of Barbarism*, pp.71-72.

(4) Pakenham: *The Boer War*, p.538.

(5) Cooperation of Dr C de Jong regarding various publications that appeared in magazines regarding executions in the Transvaal.

CHAPTER 1

(1) Compiled from articles by Tom Andrews in *Pretoriana*, No. 73 in 1977; Spies: *Methods of Barbarism*, pp.161-162.

CHAPTER 2

(1) *S.A. Biografiese Woordeboek*, pp.491-492. Free State Archives; *Africana Notes and News*; *Optrede van Cornelis Broeksma*, pp.211-217.

(2) *Standard Encyclopedia of South Africa*, Vol. 6, p.457.

(3) Information regarding the grave of Cornelis Broeksma received from: Transvaal Archives, AG 217/09; Reitz Broeksma of Somerset West, M Broeksma of Cape Town, CA Hollenbach of Florida Park.

CHAPTER 3

(1) Based on HJ Jooste: *Christiaan de Wet Annale* No. 6; Ian Uys: *Heidelbergers of the Boer War*, (1981).

(2) HJ Jooste: *Christiaan de Wet Annale* No. 6, pp.51, 55.

(3) First verse from the poem by C Louis Leipoldt, 'Salmon van As'. Published in *Die Brandwag* on 1 May 1916, 13 years after the small tree was planted on his

grave. In 1933 this poem was included in *Uit Drie Wêrelddele*.

(4) According to Dr C de Jong in *Historia* of May 1977 and in *Scandinavians in the Anglo-Boer War*, pp.149-151; Lionel Wilson: *Rustenburgers at War*, pp.191-193; Breytenbach: *Gedenkalbum*, pp.179-181.

(5) Information from Prof. Gert van den Berg of Potchefstroom; Breytenbach: *Gedenkalbum*, p.216; Tom Andrews in *Pretoriana* No. 13 of 1977. Conan Doyle: *The War in South Africa*, p.129.

(6) Information from Mrs JA Kilian of Paarl.

(7) Information from Deon Visser, Frederikstad station on the farm Boskop.

(8) Spies: *Methods of Barbarism*, p.71.

CHAPTER 4

(1) *Die Volksblad*. Unfortunately, the date has been torn off but it would be around 1914.

(2) This saga is based on court records from the Archives in Bloemfontein: AG 4584/02; *Dagbreek en Landstem* of 12 October 1969; Spies: *Methods of Barbarism*, p.71; and the cooperation of Mr CL Pienaar of Kragbron.

(3) According to: *The History of Harrismith* by FA Steytler by kind permission of the Public Library, Harrismith. Spies: *Methods of Barbarism*, p.71.

(4) Spies: *Methods of Barbarism*, p.72; Conan Doyle: *The War in South Africa*, p.131.

(5) Transvaal Archives: CJC 840/1287.

(6) Spies: *Methods of Barbarism*, p.72; Transvaal Archives.

CHAPTER 5

(1) Information from *Heidelbergers of the Boer War* (1981) by Ian S Uys, pp.187-189.

(2) Information from Prof. MCE van Schoor.

CHAPTER 6

(1) Spies: *Methods of Barbarism*, p.35, 61-62.

(2) Article by Tom Andrews in *Pretoriana* No. 73, 1977; Spies: *Methods of Barbarism*, p.71, 240.

(3) Transvaal Archives: AG 217/09.

(4) According to Tom Andrews in *Pretoriana* No. 73, 1977; Conan Doyle: *The War in South Africa*, p.131; Spies: *Methods of Barbarism*, p.72, 240; Transvaal Archives: 217/09, U.D.J. 294/9572.

(5) According to Tom Andrews in *Pretoriana* No. 73, 1977; Conan Doyle: *The War in South Africa*, p.130; Spies: *Methods of Barbarism*, p.72, 240; Transvaal Archives: 217/09, U.D.J. 294/1522.

(6) Transvaal Archives: AG 217/09.

(7) Article by Tom Andrews in *Pretoriana* No. 13, 1977, p.3.

CHAPTER 7

(1) Based on an article in *Knapsak*, which took the form of a newsletter from the War Museum by Prof. AWG Raath printed in September 1990 as well as writings by the author.

CHAPTER 8

(1) Spies: *Methods of Barbarism*, p.60.

(2) *Historia* No. 1, May 1981, pp.41, 45, 52.

(3) Raath: *Vroue Leed*, p.94.

(4) Van Zyl: *Helde-album*, p.259.

(5) Breytenbach: *Gedenkalbum*, p.445; Van Zyl: *Helde-album*, p.391; Spies: *Methods of Barbarism*, p.291.

(6) Spies: *Methods of Barbarism*, p.277.

(7) Breytenbach: *Gedenkalbum*, p.197.

(8) Ibid pp.180-181.

(9) Ibid pp.446-447.

(10) Raath: *Vroue Leed*, Section 4.

(11) Snyman: *Rebelleverhore*, p.70.

(12) Oosthuizen: *Rebelle van die Stormberge*, pp.222, 226 and follows; Snyman: *Rebelleverhore*, p.70.

(13) Taken from the article written in *Pretoriana* No. 92 on November 1987 by Prof. A Davey, pp.45-48; *Historia* No. 1, May 1981, pp.37-58. This article was written by Dr CAR Schulenburg; Article written by Tom Andrews in *Pretoriana* No. 13, 1977, pp.9-11.

(14) Snyman: *Rebelleverhore*, p.63; according to G Preller in *Scheepers se Dagboek*, pp.99-100.

APPENDIX E

Select Bibliography

BREYTENBACH, JH *Gedenkalbum van die Tweede Vryheidsoorlog*. Published by Nasionale Pers, Cape Town, 1949.

DOYLE, ARTHUR CONAN *The war in South Africa. Its cause and conduct*. Published by Smith Edler & Co., London, 1902.

GREYLING, DR E *Tussen die Berge*. Unpublished.

JORDAAN, G *Hoe Zij Stierven*. Originally published by De Stem Drukkery, Burgersdorp, 1904.

KOTZE, PROF. HN & DA *Oorlog Sonder Oorwinning*. Published by Pastelle, Hermanus, 1999.

MEINTJIES, J *Stormberg. A Lost Opportunity*. Published by Nasionale Boekhandel, 1969.

NASSON, B *Abraham Esau's War*. Published by Cambridge University Press, 1991.

OOSTHUIZEN, AV *Rebelle van die Stormberge*. Published by JP van der Walt, Pretoria, 1992.

PAKENHAM, T *The Boer War*. Published by Jonathan Ball Publishers, Johannesburg, 1979.

PRINSLOO, A *Smithfield 1819–1962*. Published by NG Sendingpers, Bloemfontein, 1955.

PRETORIUS, F *Kommandolewe tydens die Anglo-Boereoorlog*. Published by Human & Rousseau, Cape Town, 1991.

REITZ, DENEYS *Commando*. Published by Faber & Faber, London, 1929.

SCHEEPERS-STRYDOM, CJ *Kaapland en die Tweede Vryheidsoorlog*. Published by Nasionale Pers, Cape Town.

SPIES, SB *Methods of Barbarism*. Human & Rousseau, Cape Town, 1977.

VAN ZYL, HPS *Helde-album van ons Vryheidstryd*. Published by Die Afrikaanse Pers Boekhandel, Johannesburg, 1944.

VENTER, DR EA *Ons Geskiedenisalbum*. Published by Dr EA Venter, Potchefstroom, 1983.

WARWICK, P *Black People and the South African War*. Published by Cambridge University Press, 1983.

RADLOFF, REV. CH *Gevangenis-Stemmen*. Published by H.A.U.M., Cape Town, 1903.

WRITINGS & ESSAYS

BOTHA, TA 'Graaff-Reinet tydens die Anglo-Boereoorlog.' Masters Degree with Honours. University of Port Elizabeth, 1991.

CONSTANTINE, RJ 'The Guerilla War in the Cape Colony during the South African War 1899–1902.' Masters Degree, 1989. Unpublished.

SHEARING, HA 'The Second Invasion of the Cape Colony during the Anglo-Boer War 1899–1902.' Masters Degree, 1989. Unpublished.

SNYMAN, JH 'Rebelle-verhoor in Kaapland gedurende die Tweede Vryheidsoorlog met spesiale verwysing na die Militêre Howe.' Masters Degree, 1962. Archives Year Book 1962.

SNYMAN, JH 'Die Afrikaner in Kaapland 1899–1902.' Proof writing for the degree D.Litt., 1973. Archives Year Book 1979.

RAATH, AWG 'Vroue Leed.' Published by the War Museum, Bloemfontein.

ARCHIVES

Government Blue Books in the National Archives, Cape Town.

Transvaal Archives, Records Section, Pretoria.

War Museum of the Boer Republics, Bloemfontein.

Free State Archives, Records Section, Bloemfontein.

MAGAZINES, PERIODICALS, NEWSPAPERS AND OTHER PUBLICATIONS

Brandwag, 4 June 1948.
Christiaan de Wet Annale No. 6: 'Salmon van As' by HJ Jooste.
Geskiedenis van Harrismith: FA Steytler.
Graaff-Reinet, Die Ontstaan v.d. Gemeente Nuwe Kerk: Dr S du Toit.
Graaff-Reinet Advertiser 1900–1902.
Graaff-Reinet, History of the District 1786–1901: KW Smith, Rhodes University, 1976.
Heidelbergers of the Boer War: Ian Uys.
Historia 1977, 1981: Dr C de Jong and Dr CAR Schulenburg.
Huisgenoot, 12 January 1945.
Kenhardt, History of; from Mrs Martha Jooste.
Knapsak, Newsletters from the War Museum of the Boer Republics, September 1990.
Northern Post and Border News, Aliwal North, 1900–1902.
Pretoriana No. 73 and 92: Tom Andrews and Dr C de Jong.
Rustenburgers at War: Lionel Wulfsohn.
Somerset East Budget, 25 January 1902.
Standard Encyclopedia of South Africa.
Suid Afrikaanse Biografiese Woordeboek.
Vryburg Gedenkboek.
Dagbreek en Landstem, 12 October 1969.

DIARIES

Scheepers se Dagboek, GS Preller.
Scobell se Dagboek, in the possession of Dr A van Dyk, Bloemfontein.

MUSEUMS AND PRISONS VISITED

Aberdeen
Aliwal North
Burgersdorp. The old prison is now the local commando headquarters.
Cradock. Recently destroyed by vandals. Displayed photos of the four rebels.
Colesberg
Dordrecht
Graaff-Reinet. Still being used for minor offences.
Jamestown
Mafeking
Middelburg
Molteno
Prince Albert
Somerset East
Sterkstroom
Upington
Vryburg. It is now the museum.

ASSISTANCE REGARDING INFORMATION

A grateful thanks is extended to all who made our work so much more interesting and rewarding. Without your cooperation this publication might not have been possible.

Baartman, Mrs Hermie, Graaff-Reinet Museum.
Badenhorst, Emile, Somerset East.
Botha, Dr Teo, Graaff-Reinet.
Broeksma, Reitz, Somerset West.
Broeksma, Marius, Cape Town.
Constantine, Rodney, Cape Town.
Crawley, Rina, Harrismith.
De Jong, Dr C, Faerie Glen.
De Swart, Dr J, Uitenhage.
De Villiers, Danie, Cape Town.
Du Plessis, Piet, Bloemfontein.
Du Toit, Dr Schalk, Murraysburg.
Edwards, Mrs June, Molteno Museum and Library.
Gertenbach, Jimmy, Zastron.
Gordon, Mrs Belinda, Colesberg Museum.
Greyling, Dr Paul, Pretoria.
Hattingh, Hannes, Lyttleton.
Hattingh, Rev. Hannes, Worcester.
Hollenbach, CA, Florida Park.
Jooste, Laurens, Die Wilgers, Pretoria.
Jooste, Dr Tielie, Port Elizabeth.
Jooste, Mrs Martha, Kenhardt.
Jooste, Kobus, Upington.
Kilian, Mrs JA, Paarl.
Kluyts, Mrs Mariette, Burgersdorp Cultural and Historical Museum.
Kolver, John, Grootfontein, Philippolis.
Kruger, Gerrit, Steynsburg.
Loock, Johan, Bloemfontein.
Loest, Mrs LP, Rouxville.
Marais, DJ, Bronkhorstspruit.
Meadows, Barry, Eenzaamheid, Colesberg.
Pienaar, CL and Rika, Kragbron.
Pretorius, Prof. Fransjohan, Pretoria.

Raath, Prof. AWG, Bloemfontein.
Rupping, Mrs Lettie, Rietpoort, Tarkastad.
State Archives at Bloemfontein, Cape Town and Pretoria.
Strauss, JAB, Upington.
Strydom, Hans, Brits.
Swart, Prof. Marius, Port Elizabeth.
Van den Berg, Prof. Gert, Potchefstroom.
Van der Walt, Dr Fanie, Pretoria.
Van der Walt, Albert, Somerset Printers, Somerset East.
Van der Westhuizen, Louw, De Rust.
Van Dyk, Dr Arnold, Bloemfontein.

Van Heerden, Kotie en Engela, Skaapkraal, Tarkastad.
Van Heerden, George en Estelle, Golden Valley, Tarkastad.
Van Schoor, Prof. MCE, Betty's Bay, Cape.
Van Vuuren, Jozua, Pretoria.
Van Zyl-Smit, Elsa, Pretoria.
Visser, Deon, Frederikstad.
Von Caues, Leon, Hertzogville.
Vorster, Ben, Sewefontein, Middelburg, Cape.
War Museum of the Boer Republics, Bloemfontein.